PLANK GRILLING

75 Recipes for Infusing Food with Flavor Using Wood Planks

DINA GUILLEN

Photography by Rina Jordan

SASQUATCH BOOKS
SEATTLE

To Roland and Andrew, for all the love, support, and encouragement I could ever dream of

Printed in China

Published by Sasquatch Books

18 17 16 15 14   9 8 7 6 5 4 3 2 1

Editor: Gary Luke
Project editor: Michelle Hope Anderson
Design: Anna Goldstein
Photographs: Rina Jordan
Food styling: Nathan Carrabba
Wood Texture: © Alexander Bark / Shutterstock.com
Copy editor: Erin Riggio

Library of Congress Cataloging-in-Publication Data is available.

ISBN: 978-1-57061-900-7

Sasquatch Books
1904 Third Avenue, Suite 710
Seattle, WA 98101
(206) 467-4300
www.sasquatchbooks.com
custserv@sasquatchbooks.com

CONTENTS

INTRODUCTION

One of my culinary icons, Chef Michel Richard, wrote, "In cooking, as in love, you have to try new things to keep it interesting." We all have our standbys, the same recipes we go to over and over again when we prepare grilled chicken, pork, salmon, beef, and vegetables. But to keep things interesting, we are always looking for new ways to prepare them.

This book will help you make things interesting. Yes, there's the chance your wood plank will catch on fire. But isn't that the epitome of interesting? I admit, the risk that my cedar-planked salmon might catch on fire is the reason I was highly hesitant, even intimidated, to begin plank grilling. But the opportunity to keep things interesting is always appealing to me, especially when it comes to food. Of course, once I realized that a simple spray bottle sitting next to my cooking area could extinguish flare-ups quickly, it was all anyone could do to keep me away from the grill.

This book is also designed to give you the tools to plank-grill confidently. I had the advantage of my brother's guidance during my introduction to plank grilling. He owned a company that manufactured grilling planks, and he passed along some helpful tips to get me started. Those tips and many more have made it into this book. I am not a chef, nor some master griller. I'm a professional writer with a passion for cooking, entertaining, and passing on recipes that you will hopefully crave long after you have prepared them.

I am always asked what my favorite recipes are grilled on the plank. Obviously, salmon on a cedar plank is the most popular, and for good reason. Cedar and salmon pair exceptionally well together. I have heard from countless people that their favorite salmon dishes are the ones that have been plank-grilled. And I would have to agree, but it turns out that plank-grilling a meat loaf can turn that simple dish into one of the most mouthwatering entrées you will ever eat. There are two meat loaf recipes in this book: Turkey, Sage, and Pomegranate Meat Loaf (page 115) and Meat Loaf with Tomato and Red Pepper Sauce (page 125). They'll both convert you into a meat loaf fan if you weren't one before.

In fact, plank grilling elevates most meat dishes with the infusion of wood and smoke flavors, like Pork Tenderloin with Raspberry Chipotle Sauce (page 102), Chicken Thighs with Cherry Port Sauce (page 109), or Lamb Shoulder Chops with Tamarind Apricot Glaze (page 134). The only meat I don't prefer plank-grilled is a steak, so you won't find any rib-eye or porterhouse recipes in this book. I like my steaks cooked rare on the inside and crispy and crusty on the outside, and since food requires at least ten minutes on the plank to be infused with the smoke and wood flavors, it is difficult to get that unique plank-grilled flavor and still achieve the texture I love in a steak. But because taste is so subjective, definitely feel free to throw a steak on the plank if you want to give it a try.

Here's a tip: If you're trying to get a loved one to eat their vegetables, try plank-grilling them (the vegetables, I mean, not your loved ones). Acorn Squash Glazed with Chipotle and Maple (page 148), Carrots Glazed with Molasses and Miso (page 155), and Tomato, Fennel, and Fresh Mozzarella Napoleons (page 142) are three of my favorites.

And finally, I've dedicated a whole chapter to pizzas, because when someone asks me what my favorite thing to grill on a plank is, my answer is always pizza. Plank-grilled pizzas taste like pizzas from a wood-burning oven, but instead of spending a thousand dollars to install one in your backyard, you spend approximately four dollars for a wood plank. Pizza Margherita (page 43) and Fig and Feta Pizza with Prosciutto (page 48) are two of my favorites, but honestly, you can't go wrong with any of them.

The pizza chapter is also the only chapter in the book with a few dessert recipes. S'mores Pizza (page 66) is particularly suited to plank grilling; the smoky flavor it absorbs from the plank makes me feel like I'm on a camping trip as I wipe the gooey chocolate and marshmallows from my cheeks.

I hope you love grilling from this book as much as I loved working on it. My wish is that these recipes will help you to create long, leisurely meals shared with family, friends, and loved ones, lingering over the table long into the night as you're reveling about how wonderful life is when it gets interesting. Enjoy!

WHO WALKED THE PLANK FIRST?

Although a relatively new trend in restaurants, plank grilling has actually been around for hundreds of years. This cooking method was pioneered by Native Americans in the Pacific Northwest where every summer, they held ritual ceremonies giving thanks for the annual migration of wild salmon. Native Americans believed that the salmon was a gift from the rivers and ocean, and they held huge feasts celebrating the arrival of this sacred food.

Tribes from the Pacific Northwest typically used spices only sparingly with their fresh food. Cedar wood was used for its seasoning ability to flavor food with its natural oils and smoke. Additionally, Native Americans believed in the medicinal healing powers of cedar wood and held it in very high esteem.

Traditionally, salmon fillets were tied to wood planks with sticks and vines, and leaned vertically toward a large open fire pit. The salmon roasted slowly, basted by its own juices and flavored with the licks of flames, wafts of smoke, and infusion of spicy wood. The wood worked double duty, keeping the food clean during the cooking process and eliminating the need to flick grains of sand off of the fish in addition to flavoring it.

According to plank manufacturer Great Lakes Grilling, the earliest plank-grilling recipe ever documented was written by the brilliant Fannie Farmer, and it featured plank chicken and duchess potatoes. This recipe appeared in the *Boston Cooking-School Cook Book* published in 1911 (this popular cookbook was reprinted as *The Fannie Farmer Cookbook*, which continues to be in print today).

With the invention of consumer grills in the 1950s, plank grilling became much more popular, especially with chefs around the country. Restaurants really deserve the credit for pioneering the way for home cooks, offering cedar-planked salmon on their menus year-round; many restaurants also try out new ways to use grilling planks to season other meats, fruits, cheeses, and vegetables.

The most authentically prepared cedar-planked meal you will find in a restaurant has to be at the Mitsitam Native Foods Café found inside the Smithsonian National Museum of the American Indian in Washington, DC. The café has salmon shipped from the Quinault Indian Nation and grills it in the native fashion, tied to cedar planks and cooked over an open fire. Restaurants with multiple locations nationwide where you can find delicious cedar-planked salmon on the menu include Gordon Biersch, Seasons 52, Sullivan's Steakhouse, Shari's Restaurants, and celebrity chef Guy Fieri's Johnny Garlic.

CHOOSING A PLANK

You have many choices when it comes to grilling planks. Planks come in a variety of hardwoods, sizes, and shapes. Before you go out and buy one, there are two things you'll want to consider: size and wood type. The size of the plank you choose will be based on how many people you are feeding, and the type of wood will vary depending on what you're cooking.

Most grilling planks are about ⅜ inch thick and come in rectangular shapes, roughly 15 by 7 inches. All the recipes in this book can be prepared on planks of these dimensions. Grilling planks also come in squares, ovals, and even individual serving sizes.

If those sizes don't meet your needs, or if you want to save a little money, head over to a lumberyard and purchase your own hardwood. Cut it to your preferred length and sand it to avoid getting splinters. You don't want the plank to be too thick or too thin. A plank that's too thick restricts the transfer of heat and is a waste of wood, while a plank that's too thin can burn up before your food is cooked through. A ⅜- to ½-inch-thick plank is ideal. Most importantly, make sure to let the lumberyard know that you want untreated wood. Many woods are treated to prevent mold, rot, and insect infestation, and these chemical treatments could easily be absorbed into the food.

Choose hardwoods for plank grilling since they can withstand high heat and last longer. Avoid birch, pine, and poplar woods since they infuse the food with bitter flavors. It helps to know the flavor profile of each wood so that you can choose the dish that best complements it.

WESTERN RED CEDAR is the most common wood used for plank grilling, especially for plank-grilled salmon. It has a spicy, sweet, smoky flavor; is strong and robust; and is a perfect complement to seafood, vegetables, and fruit.

ALDER imparts a more subtle flavor than cedar does. It has hints of vanilla and can be sweet and nutty. Alder pairs great with salmon, pork, chicken, turkey, and pizzas.

MAPLE is a mild wood, which makes it complementary to a lot of foods. The buttery, sweet, and smooth flavors work especially well with seafood, pork, chicken, turkey, fruit, pizzas, and quesadillas.

CHERRY is a sweet, fruity, and smoky wood. It pairs perfectly with gamier meats like lamb, duck, venison, and pheasant.

OAK has a robust, heavy, smoky flavor that makes an excellent pairing with beef and chicken.

Finally, while recommendations are made on each recipe for the best types of wood to use with each dish, they are just that—recommendations. Nothing is set in stone and there are no rules about flavor combinations. Trust your instincts and feel free to play around with woods based on your own personal taste.

HEALTHY BENEFITS
of Plank Grilling

You've probably heard the saying, "Fat is flavor." Chefs add a lot of butter and oil to restaurant dishes, giving them maximum flavor and moisture. When we cook at home, we add fat to our roasted dishes, fried dishes, sautéed dishes, even a lot of grilled dishes, just to give them that extra flavor boost and ensure moistness. Grilling on wood is a natural and healthy way of cooking because the food doesn't need any fat to be moist and flavorful—the wood plank accomplishes that. And wood has no calories.

When heat hits the surface of the plank, oils are released from the wood that flavor the food and keep it moist at the same time. As the wood begins to lightly smoke, it flavors the food with a smoky aroma usually achieved with bacon or other fatty smoked meats. This double infusion of flavor from the wood and smoke alleviates the need for any additional oils, liquids, and sauces to achieve juicier, more flavorful dishes.

In addition to less fat, less salt is needed when plank-grilling a dish as well. I always used to brine pork and turkey before cooking them, soaking them in salt, sugar, and water for hours to ensure a moist interior after grilling. There is no need for brining anymore because the wood and smoke keep the meat moist.

Lastly, there have been several medical reports suggesting that charring meat, fish, and chicken over an open flame produces a cancer-causing substance known as carcinogens. Far less charring and blackening occurs when grilling proteins on a plank, since there is a barrier between the food and the flame. When flare-ups occur, the plank gets charred—not the food—substantially reducing your risk of ingesting carcinogens.

GETTING STARTED

Not to be confused with smoked foods, plank-grilled foods have a less intense taste than smoked foods, and are cooked using a completely different method. Knowing the correct way to grill on a wood plank will help you build the confidence to try this method of cooking and wow dinner guests with the flavors and smells of a plank-grilled meal.

Will This Work with My Grill?

Whether you have a gas or charcoal grill, plank grilling can work successfully for you. I prefer gas grills because I can control the heat and flame, and as a result, most of the tips and guidelines in this book are tailored for gas grills.

If you have a charcoal grill, prepare your grill for indirect grilling, piling one side of the grill with the hot coals, and letting the other side of the grill remain cool. Start grilling on the hot side of the grill, getting your plank hot and smoky. Place your food on the plank while it is on the hot side of the grill, and only move the plank to the cool side if flare-ups occur. Use the top and bottom vents to control the amount of heat in the grill. Additional directions for plank-grilling with a charcoal grill using indirect heat can be found under Preheating the Plank on page 12.

Soaking the Plank

Start by using a clean, untreated piece of wood. Most of the wood planks sold in stores are ⅜ to 1 inch thick. Be sure to choose a plank that allows at least a 1-inch border around the food you are preparing. No matter the size, plan on soaking your plank for at least one hour, and up to twenty-four hours. This important step adds moisture that helps the wood to resist burning, which prolongs the use of your plank.

Place the plank in a kitchen sink, cooler, glass or ceramic baking dish, or any container large enough to fit it for soaking.

Soak the plank in water, or if you feel like being creative, try adding some white wine, beer, salt, or apple, berry, or citrus juice to the water.

Keep the plank submerged with something heavy, like a brick, so it stays weighted down during soaking.

Preheating the Plank

Preheating the plank before grilling is an important step. With woods like maple, oak, cherry, and alder, the plank will often begin to warp when placed over heat (cedar does not usually warp). Preheating the plank will control the warping, kill any bacteria on the cooking surface, and impart a more intense flavor to the food.

Before preheating the plank, have a spray bottle with water handy to smolder any flames if flare-ups occur.

For a gas grill, preheat your grill to medium-high, or about 400 degrees F. For a charcoal grill, prepare your grill for indirect cooking: Fill a chimney starter (charcoal chimney) to the top with charcoal. Light the charcoal and let it burn until half of the coals are glowing. Spread the coals onto half of the bottom of the grill, leaving the other side without coals (this is called the "indirect method"). Place the grill lid on top and fully open the top and bottom vents. If your grill does not have a thermometer, place a grill thermometer through one of the vent openings and let it sit for 5 minutes to get an accurate reading. If the grill gets too hot, close the vents partially

and let the temperature adjust. Continue making adjustments to the vent openings until the grill reaches a consistent temperature of 400 degrees F.

For optimum smoke and wood flavor, place the plank 8 to 12 inches above the flame and close the grill lid. I prefer to place a plank on the warming rack of my gas grill for preheating and grilling. It takes a little longer to get it lightly toasted and get some smoke going (8 to 10 minutes), but it reduces the number of flare-ups so that you will get more uses out of the plank. If the plank is placed closer to the flame, you should see some light smoke after 3 to 5 minutes. Keep a close eye on the grill if the plank is closer to the flame.

Once you see some light wisps of gray smoke emanating from the grill, open the grill lid and flip the plank over. If the plank has not bowed, you are ready to begin grilling. If warping occurs, close the lid again and continue preheating another minute or two until the plank flattens out. Continue flipping and heating the plank one or two more times until warping is controlled.

Grilling Food on the Plank

When it comes to plank grilling, smoke is your friend. Not just any old friend—it's your best friend. Without smoke, you don't get the full advantages and benefits of plank grilling. So once the food is placed on the wood and the grill lid is closed, monitoring the smoke is key. One of the most helpful tools for plank grilling is a wireless meat thermometer. It remotely monitors the internal temperature of the meat, which means you don't have to open the grill lid and release all that important smoke and heat when checking it.

Always have water nearby; a spray bottle, a hose, a cup of water—anything that can smolder flames in case the plank catches on fire.

Start by placing the food on the toasted side of the preheated plank. Unless the recipe states otherwise, you always want to place the food in a single layer, maximizing the absorption and infusion of the wood into the food.

Close the grill lid and vigilantly monitor the smoke. If the smoke dissipates while the food is being placed on the plank, raise the heat until you begin to see a light gray to white smoke emanating from the grill. For a charcoal grill, open vents as required to increase the temperature. Once the smoke is a light gray, lower the heat so that it doesn't become billowing black smoke (which could mean your plank is on fire!).

Keep monitoring the smoke throughout the grilling process to maintain that light gray color. You will notice there are no grilling temperatures in the recipes. That's because the temperature at which you attain that light gray smoke is the temperature you want to be at for the duration of grilling. Recipes do, however, provide the length of time it takes to grill your dish. The grilling times are based on light gray smoke being consistent around 400 degrees F. But each grill is different, so don't rely on the thermometer as much as your eyes. Sometimes smoke will be consistent at 350 degrees F, sometimes at 450 degrees F. Let the color of the smoke be your guide.

Unless the recipe states otherwise, keep the grill lid closed throughout the grilling process. Think of your grill as an oven—every time you open it, heat escapes and flavor diminishes. With plank grilling, you have the added risk of a fire starting from the air entering the heated space. It is the most difficult part of plank grilling, but don't be tempted to peek. Let the natural humidity of the wood envelop the dish, let the smoke work its magic, and the results will be worth it! If you are plank-grilling meat, a wireless meat thermometer is incredibly helpful and highly recommended.

Don't flip the food while grilling on the plank. It's like trying to flip a loaf of bread baking in the oven—there's no need. The plank method ensures even cooking

When the food is done grilling and has been transferred to a serving platter, soak the hot plank in a container of water. A cooler is ideal, since it can be placed at the ready near the grill and is large enough to hold a lot of water.

Reusing and Cleaning the Plank

Planks can be reused anywhere from two to four times. If salmon or any other fish was grilled on the plank, it is best to reuse that plank for fish only to prevent fishy flavors from being absorbed into your next plank-grilled meal.

After each use, scrub your plank down with water and a brush without soap, and let the plank air-dry completely to prevent molding.

Store used planks in paper bags or cardboard boxes until the next use.

Soak and preheat used planks just like you would new planks.

Once the plank is completely charred after a few uses, crumble it and spread on the bottom of the grill to use as smoking chips.

14 Things You
Should Know Before
PLANK
GRILLING

1. There are two types of wood planks sold in stores: grilling planks and baking planks. Baking planks typically cost four or five times as much as grilling planks, are designed for the oven, and will last for years. Grilling planks are manufactured for the grill and only last for about two to four uses. The two are not interchangeable.

2. Check lumberyards for leftover wood they may not need. A lot of times they won't charge you, but if they do, it will probably be a lot less than buying packaged planks from the store. Just make sure it is untreated wood.

3. Gas grills vary widely in wattage and performance. If your grill is new, test-drive it a few times so there are no surprises when you place the wood planks over the flames.

4. Always clean the grill well before placing a wood plank on the grates to minimize flare-ups from remnants of previously grilled food.

5. Make sure all meat is at room temperature (let sit for about thirty minutes, longer for thicker cuts) before placing it on the plank to ensure even grilling and reduce the risk of the meat drying out.

6. Be organized. Prepare sauces, rubs, and sautés; measure out all ingredients; and have everything arranged by the grill before you place the food on the plank. Once you open the lid, quickly plank the food and close the grill lid to minimize the loss of heat and smoke.

7. Never leave your grill unattended. Once the plank is on the grill, stay close by in case there are flare-ups that need to be extinguished.

8. Cooking times will vary depending on the grill, plank placement, plank thickness, and amount of food on the plank. Extra time will be needed if recipes are doubled or additional items are added while grilling.

9. A constant light gray smoke is the key to plank grilling, so avoid opening the grill lid whenever possible. A wireless meat thermometer is helpful since it remotely monitors the internal temperature of the food.

10. Be careful when removing the plank from the grill, as it will have absorbed heat during cooking. Use potholders or oven gloves when handling it.

11. Allow beef, pork, chicken, lamb, and other meats to rest for at least ten minutes (longer for thick cuts of meat) after removing them from the grill. This gives the meat's juices a chance to be reabsorbed rather than lost on your plate.

12. For a beautiful presentation, you can serve a food directly from the plank if it is not too charred. Just remember to protect the table surface from the plank heat by placing it on a heatproof tray, platter, or trivet.

13. To save time, soak the plank, wrap it in a plastic bag, and store it in the freezer. That way it is ready to be used the next time you want to plank-grill. Used planks can be cleaned, soaked, and stored in the freezer up to two months.

14. Keep track of what kind of food you used a plank for, and only use it in the future to prepare the same type of food, especially seafood. This helps prevent fishy or other strong flavors from being absorbed into your next plank-grilled meal.

STARTERS & SOUPS

Bacon-Wrapped Dates Stuffed with
Blue Cheese and Pecans 21

Beet Hummus 23

Sausage-Stuffed Mushrooms 24

Corn Guacamole 25

Scotch Eggs with Mustard
Sauce 26

Salmon Chowder 29

Tomato Bisque 30

Butternut Squash and Apple Soup
with Spiced Pumpkin Seeds 31

Green Chile Chowder 34

Red Pepper and
Tarragon Soup 36

The starters in this chapter are twists on classic recipes—after being plank-grilled, they deliver huge flavor and may convert you to this new way of preparing them. Try the Bacon-Wrapped Dates Stuffed with Blue Cheese and Pecans (page 21) and Beet Hummus (page 23) to see what I mean.

I love making soup. Served in small cups or tiny bowls, it makes the ideal start to a meal. Alongside crusty bread and a nice side salad, it's a perfect meal in itself. Best of all, I love making soup for dinner parties because it can be made ahead and then warmed right before serving. Plank-grilling ingredients before adding them to a soup seasons it with the aroma of smoke and the flavors of wood. Most of the soups in this chapter are vegetarian-friendly and can be prepared with water or vegetable stock. The Tomato Bisque (page 30) and Green Chile Chowder (page 34) are two of my favorites.

Bacon-Wrapped Dates Stuffed with Blue Cheese and Pecans

This appetizer hits all the right notes: salty, sweet, smoky, sticky, crispy, and creamy. With that combination of flavors and textures, this is one of my favorite go-to starters. The fact that these delicious morsels can sit at room temperature for a few hours after grilling and still taste unbelievably luscious is just another reason to love them. In case you needed another reason to love a dish wrapped in bacon.

PLANK PREFERENCE: Cedar

MAKES 15 STUFFED DATES, SERVING 4 TO 6 AS AN APPETIZER

2 tablespoons maple syrup
⅛ teaspoon cayenne pepper
15 large (1¼-inch-long) soft Medjool dates
1¼ ounces blue cheese, crumbled (about ¼ cup)
15 pecan halves
5 slices bacon, each cut into 3 equal pieces
15 toothpicks

• Soak the plank for at least 1 hour and up to 24 hours.

• In a small bowl, stir together the maple syrup and cayenne. Set aside.

• Cut a lengthwise slit in each date and carefully remove the pit, forming a pocket. Fill each date with ½ teaspoon of the blue cheese and a pecan half. Wrap a piece of bacon around each stuffed date, secure with a toothpick, and brush with the maple syrup mixture.

• Prepare the plank for grilling according to the instructions on page 12. Place the dates on the toasted side of the plank. Close the lid and grill for 15 to 20 minutes, or until the bacon is crisp and the cheese has melted. Serve warm or at room temperature.

Beet Hummus

Many people are only familiar with beets that have come out of a can and confidently believe beets taste awful because they have an "earthy" flavor to them. But grilling fresh beets on a cedar plank gives them a spicy, smoky flavor that really complements their natural sweetness, eliminating that earthy flavor and bringing out the best in them. In fact, they make a great side dish just on their own, drizzled with a little lemon juice and extra-virgin olive oil. This spicy dip is a great way to showcase the beet, and if you let it sit overnight, the flavors develop even more fully. Serve with cucumber slices or toasted pita crisps.

• Soak the plank for at least 1 hour and up to 24 hours.

• Cut the beets in half and toss with the oil, ½ teaspoon of the salt, and ¼ teaspoon of the pepper.

• Prepare the plank for grilling according to the instructions on page 12. Place the beets, cut side down, on the toasted side of the plank. Close the lid and grill for 20 to 25 minutes, or until tender. Remove from the heat and set aside to cool. Once the beets are cool enough to handle, roughly chop them and place them in the bowl of a food processor.

• Add the garbanzo beans, garlic, tahini, lemon juice, cumin, coriander, red pepper flakes, and the remaining ½ teaspoon salt and ¼ teaspoon pepper to the food processor. Blend until smooth, 20 to 30 seconds. Garnish with the parsley or pine nuts.

PLANK PREFERENCE: Cedar

MAKES 2 CUPS

3 small beets (about 1 pound), trimmed and peeled

1 tablespoon extra-virgin olive oil

1 teaspoon kosher salt, divided

½ teaspoon freshly ground black pepper, divided

1 (15.5-ounce) can garbanzo beans, rinsed and drained

2 cloves garlic, chopped

3 tablespoons tahini

Juice of 1 large lemon (about 3 tablespoons)

½ teaspoon ground cumin

½ teaspoon ground coriander

¼ teaspoon crushed red pepper flakes

1 tablespoon chopped fresh flat-leaf parsley, or 1 tablespoon toasted pine nuts, for garnish (optional)

Sausage-Stuffed Mushrooms

PLANK PREFERENCE: Cedar

MAKES 20 STUFFED MUSHROOMS, SERVING 8 TO 10 AS AN APPETIZER

20 extra-large white mushrooms
¼ cup extra-virgin olive oil
3 tablespoons dry sherry
2 cloves garlic, minced
½ pound bulk Italian pork
    sausage
½ cup panko
¼ cup freshly grated Parmesan
¼ cup chopped pimento-stuffed
    olives
¼ cup chopped fresh flat-leaf
    parsley
2 tablespoons currants
½ teaspoon kosher salt
¼ teaspoon freshly ground black
    pepper

Mushrooms have an earthy flavor that works well with smoke and wood. Stuff them with sausage and you have an appetizer that is a big crowd-pleaser—they are always the first to go at parties. Make sure to include the currants; their sweetness perfectly balances the smokiness of the sausage and mushrooms. For some spice, choose a spicy Italian sausage.

◆ Soak the plank for at least 1 hour and up to 24 hours.

◆ Remove the stems from the mushrooms and chop them finely, reserving the mushroom caps. Place the chopped stems in a large bowl.

◆ In a separate large bowl, whisk together the oil, sherry, and garlic. Add the mushroom caps and toss them with the oil mixture. Set aside to marinate while you prepare the stuffing.

◆ Add the sausage, panko, Parmesan, olives, parsley, currants, salt, and pepper to the chopped mushroom stems and mix well. Fill each mushroom cap with 1 tablespoon of the sausage mixture. (The stuffed mushrooms can be prepared a day ahead: Cover and chill, then remove from the refrigerator 30 minutes before grilling to allow the mushrooms to come to room temperature.)

◆ Prepare the plank for grilling according to the instructions on page 12. Place the stuffed mushrooms, cap side down, on the toasted side of the plank. Close the lid and grill for 20 to 25 minutes, or until the sausage is cooked through and looks browned and crusty.

Corn Guacamole

I made this for a dinner party one night, and the whole bowl was devoured before I had a chance to get dinner on the table. This is a great recipe because it can be prepared ahead of time, allowing the smokiness from the grilled corn and red onion to infuse into the dip as it sits. The best type of avocado to use is the dark, thick-skinned Hass variety. Serve with corn chips for dipping.

PLANK PREFERENCE: Cedar

MAKES 6 SERVINGS

2 ears corn, husks and silk removed
½ large red onion, cut into ¼-inch-thick slices
2 large ripe avocados
1 jalapeño, seeded and finely chopped
2 tablespoons extra-virgin olive oil
1½ tablespoons light mayonnaise
Juice of 1 large lime (about 2 tablespoons)
¼ cup chopped fresh cilantro
1 teaspoon kosher salt
¼ teaspoon freshly ground black pepper

♦ Soak the plank for at least 1 hour and up to 24 hours.

♦ Prepare the plank for grilling according to the instructions on page 12. Place the corn and onion on the toasted side of the plank. Close the lid and grill for 15 minutes, or until the vegetables are tender when pierced with a knife. Remove the vegetables from the heat and set aside to cool. When the corn is cool, cut the kernels off the cob. When the onion is cool, roughly chop it.

♦ Meanwhile, peel the avocados, discard the pits, place them in a medium bowl, and mash with a fork. Add the corn, onion, jalapeño, oil, mayonnaise, lime juice, cilantro, salt, and pepper and mix well. If not serving immediately, place plastic wrap directly on the surface of the dip, and refrigerate for up to 4 hours.

Scotch Eggs with Mustard Sauce

PLANK PREFERENCE: Maple

MAKES 6 SERVINGS AS AN APPETIZER

6 large eggs
1 teaspoon rubbed dried sage
1 teaspoon kosher salt
½ teaspoon freshly ground black pepper
½ teaspoon ground nutmeg
¼ cup all-purpose flour
1 large egg, beaten
1 tablespoon milk
1 tablespoon Dijon mustard
1 cup panko
1 pound bulk Italian pork sausage

For the sauce:
¼ cup mayonnaise
1 tablespoon Dijon mustard
1 tablespoon whole grain mustard

If you walk into a pub in Scotland, the chances of finding Scotch eggs on the menu are pretty high. They are a favorite pub meal along with a cold drink, and while they look complicated, they are incredibly easy to make. A Scotch egg is essentially a hard-boiled egg wrapped in sausage and fried or baked. In this case, they are plank-grilled, and the flavors of wood and smoke infused into this classic dish transforms it into something really special. I've had friends say that the eggs are so perfect on their own, they prefer them without the sauce, but I love the kick you get from the mustard. It's your call.

◆ Soak the plank for at least 1 hour and up to 24 hours.

◆ Place the eggs in a saucepan large enough to hold them in a single layer and cover them with cold water by 1 inch. Bring the water to a boil over high heat. Turn off the heat and let sit for 12 minutes. Drain the water from the pan and fill again with cold water to cover the eggs. Once the eggs have cooled, about 10 minutes, drain the water and peel the eggs.

◆ In a small bowl, combine the sage, salt, pepper, and nutmeg.

◆ Set up an assembly line of 3 pie plates. In the first pie plate, combine the flour and ¾ teaspoon of the sage mixture. In the second pie plate, whisk together the beaten egg, milk, mustard, and ½ teaspoon of the sage mixture. In the third pie plate, combine the panko with the remaining 1¾ teaspoons sage mixture.

• Divide the sausage into 6 equal portions (about ¼ cup sausage per portion) and pat each one into a flat disc. Roll an egg in the flour mixture, then gently wrap a sausage patty around it, pinching the seams to seal the egg inside. Roll the sausage-wrapped egg in the flour mixture a second time, then in the egg mixture, then in the panko mixture. Repeat with each egg and let the prepared eggs sit for 10 minutes before grilling.

• Meanwhile, make the mustard sauce. In a small bowl, combine the mayonnaise and mustards and set aside.

• Prepare the plank for grilling according to the instructions on page 12. Place the eggs on the toasted side of the plank. Close the lid and grill for 20 to 25 minutes, or until the sausage is crisp and cooked through. Slice each egg into quarters and serve with the mustard sauce.

Salmon Chowder

My friend Laura's husband, Brock Howell, had just flown in from Seattle on business when the two of them came over for dinner. As he was eating this chowder, he told me he had just had a bowl of salmon chowder that day in Seattle, and this version was better because of the cedar and smoke flavoring. Salmon and cedar are a match made in heaven, and the combination gives this chowder a real "wow" factor.

• Soak the plank for at least 1 hour and up to 24 hours.

• First, prepare the salmon. In a small bowl, combine the salt, pepper, thyme, garlic powder, onion powder, and celery seed. Rub liberally onto the flesh side of the salmon.

• Prepare the plank for grilling according to the instructions on page 12. Place the salmon, skin side down, on the toasted side of the plank. Close the lid and grill for 10 to 15 minutes, or until the salmon is flaky around the edges but still opaque in the center. Once it has cooled slightly, remove the skin, gently break the salmon into small chunks and set aside.

• Next, prepare the chowder. Heat the milk in a medium saucepan over low heat until it is nearly simmering; do not let it boil. Meanwhile, melt the butter in a 3- to 4-quart heavy saucepan over medium heat. Add the onion, salt, and pepper and cook, stirring occasionally, until the onions are soft and translucent, about 5 minutes. Stir in the flour and cook for 3 minutes, stirring often. Whisk in the heated milk until the mixture is smooth, then add the potatoes. Increase the heat to medium-high and cook until the potatoes are just tender, about 10 minutes. Add the salmon chunks and dill and simmer just until heated through, about 2 minutes.

PLANK PREFERENCE: Cedar

MAKES 4 SERVINGS AS AN ENTRÉE, 6 AS AN APPETIZER

For the salmon:
1 teaspoon kosher salt
¼ teaspoon freshly ground black pepper
¼ teaspoon dried thyme
¼ teaspoon garlic powder
¼ teaspoon onion powder
⅛ teaspoon celery seed
1 (1 pound) salmon fillet, skin on

. . . .

5 cups whole milk
¼ cup unsalted butter
1 medium onion, finely chopped
1 teaspoon kosher salt
¼ teaspoon freshly ground black pepper
3 tablespoons all-purpose flour
2 medium russet potatoes (about 1 pound), peeled and cut into ¼-inch cubes
2 tablespoons snipped fresh dill

Tomato Bisque

MAKES 4 SERVINGS AS AN
ENTRÉE, 6 AS AN APPETIZER

6 plum tomatoes (about 1½
    pounds), halved
1 tablespoon extra-virgin olive oil
1 large onion, chopped
3 cloves garlic, minced
1½ teaspoons kosher salt
¼ teaspoon freshly ground black
    pepper
1 quart low-sodium vegetable
    stock or water
½ cup heavy cream
¼ cup chopped fresh flat-leaf
    parsley

Tomato soup is the ultimate comfort food—especially with a grilled cheese sandwich. This version is like nothing you've had before. The tomatoes soak up the flavors of smoke and wood, and you'll taste that smoky comfort in every bite. Cedar and alder woods are my favorites with this soup, but feel free to experiment and discover your own.

◆ Soak the plank for at least 1 hour and up to 24 hours.

◆ Prepare the plank for grilling according to the instructions on page 12. Place the tomato halves, cut side down, in a single layer on the plank. Close the lid and grill for 25 to 30 minutes, or until they are soft but still hold their shape. Place the tomatoes in a large bowl.

◆ Heat the oil in a 3- to 4-quart heavy saucepan over medium-high heat. Add the onion and garlic and sauté until soft and translucent, about 3 minutes. Add the tomatoes, along with any juices that have collected in the bowl. Add the salt, pepper, and stock and bring to a simmer. Reduce the heat to low, cover, and simmer for 20 minutes.

◆ Transfer the soup to a blender and, working in 3 or 4 batches so that the steam does not cause the blender lid to pop off, puree until smooth. Pass the soup through a fine-mesh sieve before returning it to the saucepan. At this point, the soup can be cooled and refrigerated for up to 2 days. Before serving, warm over medium-high heat, stirring occasionally, for 3 to 5 minutes. Remove the pot from the heat and stir in the cream and parsley.

Butternut Squash and Apple Soup with Spiced Pumpkin Seeds

Plank-grilling the butternut squash intensifies its sweetness, as it caramelizes while grilling, and Granny Smith apples lend a sweet-tart flavor to this soup that really balances the flavors of the smoke. If you don't have the time to make the spiced pumpkin seeds, my friend Lisa Berman Edmunds likes to top this soup with salted roasted pumpkin seeds, a great time-saving idea that still gives you that crunchy textural contrast.

• Soak the plank for at least 1 hour and up to 24 hours.

• First, prepare the pumpkin seeds. Preheat the oven to 250 degrees F. Lightly coat a baking sheet with the cooking spray.

• In a small bowl, combine the sugar, garlic powder, onion powder, salt, curry powder, thyme, and cayenne. In a medium bowl, toss the pumpkin seeds with the melted butter. Add the spice mixture and toss to coat the seeds thoroughly. Spread the seeds in a single layer on the prepared baking sheet. Roast for 30 minutes, stirring every 10 minutes, until the seeds are lightly browned and crunchy. Once the seeds have cooled, they can be stored in an airtight container for up to 1 week at room temperature or up to 1 month in the refrigerator.

• Prepare the plank for grilling according to the instructions on page 12. Place the squash on the toasted side of the plank. Close the lid and grill for 25 minutes, or until the squash is tender when pierced with a knife. Let the

continued

For the pumpkin seeds:

Olive oil cooking spray

1 tablespoon sugar

2 teaspoons garlic powder

2 teaspoons onion powder

1 teaspoon kosher salt

½ teaspoon curry powder

½ teaspoon dried thyme powder

⅛ teaspoon cayenne pepper

⅓ cup hulled pumpkin seeds (also called *pepitas*)

1 tablespoon unsalted butter, melted

. . . .

1 butternut squash (about 2 pounds), peeled, quartered, and seeded

2 tablespoons unsalted butter

1 medium yellow onion, chopped

2 Granny Smith apples (about ¾ pound), peeled, cored, and cut into ½-inch dice

1 teaspoon ground coriander

1 teaspoon kosher salt

¼ teaspoon freshly ground black pepper

1 quart low-sodium chicken or vegetable stock

squash sit at room temperature until it is cool enough to handle, about 20 minutes, then roughly chop it and place in a large bowl.

◆ Next, prepare the soup. Melt the butter in a 3- to 4-quart heavy saucepan over medium-high heat. Add the onion and sauté until softened, about 5 minutes. Add the apples, coriander, salt, and pepper and cook, stirring occasionally, until the spices are fragrant, about 1 minute. Add the stock and chopped squash and bring to a simmer. Reduce the heat to medium, cover, and simmer gently for 20 minutes.

◆ Transfer the soup to a blender and, working in 3 or 4 batches so that the steam does not cause the blender lid to pop off, puree until smooth. Pass the soup through a fine-mesh sieve before returning it to the saucepan. At this point, the soup can be cooled and refrigerated for up to 2 days. Before serving, warm over medium-high heat, stirring occasionally, for 3 to 5 minutes.

◆ Ladle the warm soup into bowls and garnish with the spiced pumpkin seeds.

Green Chile Chowder

PLANK PREFERENCE: Cedar

MAKES 4 SERVINGS AS AN ENTRÉE, 6 AS AN APPETIZER

6 poblano chiles, stemmed, halved, and seeded
1 tablespoon extra-virgin olive oil
1 large onion, chopped
4 cloves garlic, finely chopped
1 teaspoon kosher salt
½ teaspoon ground cumin
¼ teaspoon freshly ground black pepper
1 quart low-sodium chicken or vegetable stock
Juice of 1 large lime (about 2 tablespoons)
Grated sharp cheddar, for garnish

One of my favorite restaurants in Northern California is Duarte's Tavern in Pescadero. I can't visit this wonderful restaurant without ordering their cream of green chile soup. Since I can't get to Duarte's Tavern every time I'm craving this dish, I make my own by grilling poblano chiles on a cedar plank. This version is so creamy after pureeing that I do not add any actual cream. Instead, I love the flavor of sharp cheddar cheese melting in the soup, leaving a creamy flavor that really complements the green chiles. Adding lime juice just before serving gives this soup a nice freshness.

◆ Soak the plank for at least 1 hour and up to 24 hours.

◆ Prepare the plank for grilling according to the instructions on page 12. Place the poblano chile halves, cut side down, on the toasted side of the plank, overlapping them if necessary. Close the lid and grill for 15 minutes, or until the poblanos are crisp-tender and lightly charred. Place the poblanos in a large bowl and cover with plastic wrap. Let the poblanos sit for 10 minutes; this will loosen their skins. Rub the skins off with your fingers and discard. Roughly chop the poblanos and return them to the bowl with any juices that were released.

◆ Heat the oil in a 3- to 4-quart heavy saucepan over medium-high heat. Add the onion, garlic, salt, cumin, and pepper and sauté until the onions begin to soften, about 3 minutes. Add the stock and chopped poblanos and bring the soup to a boil. Reduce the heat to medium, cover, and simmer gently for 20 minutes.

◆ Transfer the soup to a blender and, working in 3 or 4 batches so that the steam does not cause the blender lid to pop off, puree until smooth. Pass the soup through a fine-mesh sieve before returning it to the saucepan. At this point, the soup can be cooled and refrigerated for up to 2 days. Before serving, warm the soup over medium-high heat, stirring occasionally, for 3 to 5 minutes. Remove the pot from the heat and stir in the lime juice.

◆ Ladle the warm soup into bowls and garnish with the grated cheese.

NOTE: Poblano chiles are fresh green chiles that vary in spiciness, from mild to medium-hot. They are perfect for grilling because they are thick-skinned and can withstand a lot of heat. Grilling brings out their fruity flavors as well.

Red Pepper and Tarragon Soup

PLANK PREFERENCE: Cedar

MAKES 4 SERVINGS AS AN ENTRÉE, 6 AS AN APPETIZER

4 large red bell peppers,
    stemmed, halved, and seeded
2 tablespoons extra-virgin olive oil
1 medium onion, diced
4 cloves garlic, minced
1 cup diced celery
1 large russet potato, peeled and
    cut into 1-inch dice
1¼ teaspoons kosher salt
½ teaspoon freshly ground black
    pepper
1 quart low-sodium vegetable
    stock
2 tablespoons chopped fresh
    tarragon, plus more leaves for
    garnish
¼ cup sour cream
Juice of ½ large lime (about
    1 tablespoon)

This creamy soup is perfect for a dinner party or midweek meal because it can be made in advance. Refrigerate the soup for up to 2 days, then gently reheat it and add the sour cream garnish before serving. While the dollop of lime-flavored sour cream makes a beautiful presentation, it also adds brightness and brings the rest of the ingredients into focus.

◆ Soak the plank for at least 1 hour and up to 24 hours.

◆ Prepare the plank for grilling according to the instructions on page 12. Place the bell peppers on the toasted side of the plank, cut side down, overlapping them if necessary. Close the lid and grill for 20 minutes, or until the peppers are tender and the skins are charred. Place the peppers in a large bowl and cover with plastic wrap. Let the peppers sit for 10 minutes; this will loosen their skins. Rub the skins off with your fingers and discard. Roughly chop the peppers and return them to the bowl with any juices that were released.

◆ Heat the oil in a 3- to 4-quart heavy saucepan over medium-high heat. Add the onion, garlic, celery, potato, salt, and pepper and sauté until the vegetables have softened, about 7 to 10 minutes. Add the stock and chopped peppers and bring the soup to a boil. Reduce the heat to medium, cover, and simmer gently for 25 minutes, or until the potatoes are tender.

◆ Transfer the soup to a blender and, working in 3 or 4 batches so that the steam does not cause the blender lid to pop off, puree until smooth. Pass the soup through a fine-mesh sieve before returning it to the saucepan. At this point, the soup can be cooled and refrigerated for up to 2 days. Before serving, warm over medium-high heat, stirring occasionally, for 3 to 5 minutes. Remove the pot from the heat and stir in the tarragon.

◆ In a small bowl, combine the sour cream and lime juice. Ladle the warm soup into bowls, add a dollop of the sour cream mixture in the center of each bowl, and garnish with additional tarragon leaves.

PIZZAS ON THE PLANK

Pizza Margherita 43

Barbecued Chicken Pizza 44

Peach and Prosciutto
Pizza with Arugula 47

Fig and Feta Pizza with
Prosciutto 48

Pineapple, Jalapeño, and
Pancetta Pizza 49

Pizza with Caramelized Onions,
Pear, and Gorgonzola 51

Pulled Pork and Mango Pizza 53

Sherried Linguica, Grape, and
Gorgonzola Pizza 54

Grilled Shrimp, Artichoke,
and Pesto Pizza 56

Roasted Acorn Squash,
Caramelized Onion, and
Goat Cheese Pizza 59

Pizza with Potatoes,
Caramelized Onions, Pancetta,
and Goat Cheese 61

Corn, Chorizo, and
Poblano Pizza 63

Caramel Apple Pizza 65

S'mores Pizza 66

Peach Cobbler Pizza 68

On the weekends, I love to host dinner parties. Once I discovered how amazing pizzas taste when made on the plank, those parties started to materialize during the week as well. Gatherings are so much more fun and informal when friends can eat their meals with their hands while they're chatting, and these pizzas are the perfect finger food.

The key to making these pizzas is to have everything ready before they go on the grill. I can't stress this enough, because once the dough is ready, there is no time to mince garlic or shred cheese. Having all of the ingredients on a tray by the grill, ready to top your crust, will make the process seamless. And don't be afraid to use your hands to sprinkle the toppings evenly and quickly. They are your best tools, getting the job done quickly and efficiently so you can minimize loss of smoke and heat.

All of the pizzas in this chapter are thin-crust pizzas. Whether you choose to use high-quality store-bought dough or your favorite homemade recipe, be sure to roll it out thinly. These pizzas have a rustic, crisp, lightly blistered, perfectly chewy quality, with a hint of wood and smoke. The smoke allows the flavors of the toppings to emerge, unlocking their full potential. But it is really the flavor of the wood that transforms the plank-grilled pizza from just a pizza to a really spectacular dish. The aroma of the wood infuses the pizza with an essence that cannot be achieved on a pizza stone or directly on the grill.

Grilling pizza on a plank also adds an element of versatility. Many people are intimidated by the thought of placing dough directly on a grill, concerned that it will fall through the grates. The dough is placed directly on a wood plank, eliminating those concerns and creating a perfect wood-fired oven, at a fraction of the cost of a traditional pizza oven. The plank can be re-used three to six more times, or until it starts to fall apart.

Finally, and perhaps most importantly to those with a sweet tooth, this is the only chapter with desserts. The S'mores Pizza (page 66) is my favorite. Prepare to be transported to a childhood camping trip as you eat that one.

Pizza Margherita

Sometimes the simplest things are the best. I love making this pizza in late summer when tomatoes are at their ripest. You can use any type of tomato on this pizza; they all taste wonderful when they're in season. The tomatoes soak up the flavor of the smoke better than any other vegetable or fruit and transform this pizza from something simple to something simply spectacular.

• Soak the plank for at least 1 hour and up to 24 hours.

• In a small bowl, mix 2 tablespoons of the olive oil with the garlic, salt, and pepper. Set aside.

• On a well-floured surface, roll out the pizza dough as thinly as possible into a rectangle slightly larger than the plank you are using.

• Prepare the plank for grilling according to the instructions on page 12. Lightly spray the toasted side of the plank with the cooking spray and dust with cornmeal. Place the pizza dough on the prepared plank, folding up the edges so that the dough is the same size as the plank. Lightly prick the dough all over with a fork. Close the lid and grill for 5 to 7 minutes, or until the pizza dough is lightly browned and crisp.

• Open the grill lid and brush the oil mixture evenly over the pizza dough. Lay the mozzarella slices on top of the crust, then the tomato slices. Close the lid and grill until the cheese is golden and bubbly and the tomatoes are cooked through, about 5 minutes. Transfer the pizza to a clean work surface. Drizzle with the remaining 1 tablespoon of oil, sprinkle with the basil, and season with additional salt and pepper to taste.

PLANK PREFERENCE:
Alder or Maple

MAKES 4 SERVINGS

3 tablespoons extra-virgin olive oil, divided
1 clove garlic, minced
½ teaspoon kosher salt
¼ teaspoon freshly ground black pepper
½ pound store-bought or home-made pizza dough, at room temperature
Olive oil cooking spray
Coarse grind cornmeal, for sprinkling
6 ounces fresh mozzarella, cut into ¼-inch-thick slices
1 large tomato (about 6 ounces), cut into ¼-inch-thick slices
5 large fresh basil leaves, sliced chiffonade (see note)

NOTE: To slice chiffonade means to cut leafy herbs and greens into thin ribbons. For basil, stack the leaves one on top of another, roll them up lengthwise like a cigar, and, with a sharp knife, slice them crosswise into thin strips.

Barbecued Chicken Pizza

MAKES 4 SERVINGS

1 tablespoon extra-virgin olive oil

1 (6-ounce) boneless, skinless chicken breast

¼ teaspoon kosher salt

¼ teaspoon freshly ground black pepper

½ cup barbecue sauce (I use Sweet Baby Ray's Barbecue Sauce), divided

½ pound store-bought or home-made pizza dough, at room temperature

Olive oil cooking spray

Coarse grind cornmeal, for sprinkling

3 ounces mozzarella, grated (about 1 cup)

3 ounces Gouda, grated (about 1 cup)

½ small red onion, thinly sliced (about ½ cup)

2 green onions, sliced

2 tablespoons chopped fresh cilantro

Forget those cardboard-textured, flavorless frozen barbecued chicken pizzas from the grocery store. After seeing how easy—and flavorful—it is to make your own, my hope is that you never go back. The thin crust gets nice and crisp on the wood plank and the smoke infuses the toppings with an irresistible fragrance. I prefer a sweet, molasses-based barbecue sauce, which works especially well with the smoke and wood flavors.

◆ Soak the plank for at least 1 hour and up to 24 hours.

◆ Heat the oil in a heavy medium skillet over medium-high heat. Season the chicken with the salt and pepper and sauté just until it is cooked through, about 5 minutes per side. Transfer the chicken to a cutting board and let rest for 5 minutes. Dice the chicken into ½-inch pieces. Transfer the chicken to a medium bowl and toss with ¼ cup of the barbecue sauce.

◆ On a well-floured surface, roll out the pizza dough as thinly as possible into a rectangle slightly larger than the plank you are using.

◆ Prepare the plank for grilling according to the instructions on page 12. Lightly spray the toasted side of the plank with the cooking spray and dust with cornmeal. Place the pizza dough on the prepared plank, folding up the edges so that the dough is the same size as the plank. Lightly prick the dough all over with a fork. Close the lid and grill for 5 to 7 minutes, or until the pizza dough is lightly browned and crisp.

◆ Open the grill lid and spread the remaining ¼ cup of barbecue sauce evenly over the pizza dough. Sprinkle with the mozzarella and Gouda, spoon the chicken and sauce mixture over the cheese, and scatter the red onion over the chicken. Close the lid and grill until the cheese is golden and bubbly and the chicken and onion are warmed through, about 5 minutes. Transfer the pizza to a clean work surface and sprinkle with the green onions and cilantro.

Peach and Prosciutto Pizza with Arugula

Celebrity chef Michael Chiarello has a recipe for a warm peach and prosciutto salad that I absolutely love. I decided to try converting it into a pizza, and it is so beyond satisfying. The key is using a fresh, ripe peach.

PLANK PREFERENCE:
Alder or Maple

MAKES 4 SERVINGS

• Soak the plank for at least 1 hour and up to 24 hours.

• In a small bowl, combine 2 tablespoons of the oil with the thyme, salt, and pepper. Set aside.

• On a well-floured surface, roll out the pizza dough as thinly as possible into a rectangle slightly larger than the plank you are using.

• Prepare the plank for grilling according to the instructions on page 12. Lightly spray the toasted side of the plank with the cooking spray and dust with cornmeal. Place the pizza dough on the prepared plank, folding up the edges so that the dough is the same size as the plank. Lightly prick the dough all over with a fork. Close the lid and grill for 5 to 7 minutes, or until the pizza dough is lightly browned and crisp.

• Open the grill lid and brush the oil mixture evenly over the pizza dough, then sprinkle with the mozzarella. Add the peaches, red onion, prosciutto, and goat cheese. Close the lid and grill until the cheese is golden and bubbly and the peaches and onion are cooked through, about 5 minutes. Transfer the pizza to a clean work surface.

• In a medium bowl, combine the balsamic vinegar and the remaining 1 teaspoon of oil. Add the arugula and toss to coat the leaves with the dressing. Season with salt and pepper to taste. Top the pizza with the arugula salad.

2 tablespoons plus 1 teaspoon extra-virgin olive oil, divided
½ teaspoon chopped fresh thyme
¼ teaspoon kosher salt
¼ teaspoon freshly ground black pepper
½ pound store-bought or homemade pizza dough, at room temperature
Olive oil cooking spray
Coarse grind cornmeal, for sprinkling
6 ounces mozzarella, grated (about 2 cups)
1 large firm-ripe peach, halved, pitted, and cut into thin wedges
½ small red onion, thinly sliced (about ½ cup)
6 paper-thin slices prosciutto, torn into pieces
3 ounces goat cheese, crumbled (about ¾ cup)
1 teaspoon balsamic vinegar
2 cups loosely packed arugula

NOTE: While fresh peaches are ideal, if they are not in season when you're making this pizza, use thawed frozen peaches, thinly sliced.

Fig and Feta Pizza with Prosciutto

PLANK PREFERENCE:
Alder or Maple

MAKES 4 SERVINGS

12 dried Mission figs, soaked in boiling water for 20 minutes
1 tablespoon balsamic vinegar
2 tablespoons extra-virgin olive oil
1 garlic clove, minced
1 teaspoon fennel seeds
½ teaspoon chopped fresh rosemary
½ teaspoon kosher salt
¼ teaspoon freshly ground black pepper
½ pound store-bought or home-made pizza dough, at room temperature
Olive oil cooking spray
Coarse grind cornmeal, for sprinkling
6 ounces mozzarella, grated (about 2 cups)
½ leek, white and light green parts only, thinly sliced
1 ounce feta, crumbled (about ¼ cup)
4 thin slices prosciutto

This is one of my favorite pizzas, mostly because I am a fig fanatic and will put them on practically anything. If you're not as big a fan, however, other dried fruit can be substituted, including apricots, dates, or cherries.

◆ Soak the plank for at least 1 hour and up to 24 hours.

◆ Drain the figs and thinly slice them. Place them in a small bowl and toss with the balsamic vinegar. Set aside.

◆ In another small bowl, whisk the oil with the garlic, fennel seeds, rosemary, salt, and pepper. Set aside.

◆ On a well-floured surface, roll out the pizza dough as thinly as possible into a rectangle slightly larger than the plank you are using.

◆ Prepare the plank for grilling according to the instructions on page 12. Lightly spray the toasted side of the plank with the cooking spray and dust with cornmeal. Place the pizza dough on the prepared plank, folding up the edges so that the dough is the same size as the plank. Lightly prick the dough all over with a fork. Close the lid and grill for 5 to 7 minutes, or until the pizza dough is lightly browned and crisp.

◆ Open the grill lid and brush the oil mixture evenly over the pizza dough. Sprinkle with the mozzarella and top with the figs, leek, and feta. Close the lid and grill until the toppings are golden, about 5 minutes. Transfer the pizza to a clean work surface and drape with the prosciutto.

Pineapple, Jalapeño, and Pancetta Pizza

Fresh pineapple is best for this pizza because you don't need to worry about the extra juices from the canned variety, which can make for a soggy crust. If fresh pineapple isn't available, drain a can of pineapple as well as you can, patting the slices dry with a paper towel before cutting into small cubes. If you don't like much heat, be sure to seed the jalapeño before dicing it. To do this easily, after stemming and halving it, run a spoon down the length of the jalapeño, scooping the seeds out.

• Soak the plank for at least 1 hour and up to 24 hours.

• Line a plate with paper towels. Heat 1 teaspoon of the oil in a large skillet over medium-high heat. Add the pancetta and cook, stirring, until brown and crisp, 7 to 8 minutes. Using a slotted spoon, remove the pancetta and transfer to the lined plate.

• In a small bowl, mix the remaining 2 tablespoons of oil with the garlic, rosemary, salt, and pepper. Set aside.

• On a well-floured surface, roll out the pizza dough as thinly as possible into a rectangle slightly larger than the plank you are using.

• Prepare the plank for grilling according to the instructions on page 12. Lightly spray the toasted side of the

continued

MAKES 4 SERVINGS

2 tablespoons plus 1 teaspoon extra-virgin olive oil, divided
4 ounces pancetta, cut into ¼-inch dice (about ¾ cup)
2 cloves garlic, minced
1 teaspoon chopped fresh rosemary
¼ teaspoon kosher salt
¼ teaspoon freshly ground black pepper
½ pound store-bought or homemade pizza dough, at room temperature
Olive oil cooking spray
Coarse grind cornmeal, for sprinkling
6 ounces mozzarella, grated (about 2 cups)
¼ pineapple, cut into ¼-inch dice (about 1 cup)
1 small plum tomato, chopped
½ small jalapeño, finely diced (about ½ tablespoon)

plank with the cooking spray and dust with cornmeal. Place the pizza dough on the prepared plank, folding up the edges so that the dough is the same size as the plank. Lightly prick the dough all over with a fork. Close the lid and grill for 5 to 7 minutes, or until the pizza dough is lightly browned and crisp.

◆ Open the grill lid and brush the oil mixture evenly over the pizza dough, then sprinkle with the mozzarella. Top with the pineapple, tomato, jalapeño, and pancetta. Close the lid and grill until the cheese is golden and bubbly and the pineapple and tomato are cooked through, about 5 minutes.

Pizza with Caramelized Onions, Pear, and Gorgonzola

Many of the pizzas I create take their inspiration from salads I've enjoyed. In this case, it's an arugula salad my husband, Roland, loves, with pears, almonds, and Gorgonzola.

PLANK PREFERENCE:
Alder or Maple

MAKES 4 SERVINGS

- Soak the plank for at least 1 hour and up to 24 hours.

- Heat 1 tablespoon of the oil in a large skillet over medium-high heat. Add the onion, reduce the heat to medium, and sauté, stirring occasionally, until the onion is soft and deep golden brown, about 20 minutes. Stir in the wine, 1 tablespoon of the vinegar, and the sugar. Simmer until all of the liquid is absorbed, 3 to 4 minutes. Season with the salt and pepper and set aside.

- On a well-floured surface, roll out the pizza dough as thinly as possible into a rectangle slightly larger than the plank you are using.

- Prepare the plank for grilling according to the instructions on page 12. Lightly spray the toasted side of the plank with the cooking spray and dust with cornmeal. Place the pizza dough on the prepared plank, folding up the edges so that the dough is the same size as the plank. Lightly prick the dough all over with a fork. Close the lid and grill for 5 to 7 minutes, or until the dough is lightly browned and crisp.

continued

1 tablespoon plus 1 teaspoon extra-virgin olive oil, divided

1 large red onion, halved and thinly sliced

¼ cup dry red wine

1 tablespoon plus 1 teaspoon balsamic vinegar, divided

½ teaspoon sugar

½ teaspoon kosher salt

¼ teaspoon freshly ground black pepper

½ pound store-bought or home-made pizza dough, at room temperature

Olive oil cooking spray

Coarse grind cornmeal, for sprinkling

6 ounces mozzarella, grated (about 2 cups)

2 ounces Gorgonzola, crumbled (about ½ cup)

½ ripe pear, cored and thinly sliced

2 cups loosely packed arugula

1 tablespoon sliced almonds, toasted

◆ Open the grill lid and spread the caramelized onions over the pizza dough, then sprinkle with the mozzarella and Gorgonzola. Add a single layer of pear slices (there may be some leftover). Close the lid and grill until the cheese is golden and bubbly and the pear is cooked through, about 5 minutes. Transfer the pizza to a clean work surface.

◆ In a large bowl, combine the remaining 1 teaspoon each of oil and balsamic vinegar. Add the arugula and toss. Season with salt and pepper to taste. Top the pizza with the arugula salad and sprinkle with the almonds.

Pulled Pork and Mango Pizza

I love making pulled pork sandwiches for casual get-togethers with friends. Everybody enjoys them and they go a long way. Whenever I have leftovers, I use them to make pulled pork pizza. I've tried this pizza with apricots, peaches, nectarines, and mangos, and while they're all delectable, mangos are my family's favorite. If you're not in the mood to make pulled pork, grocery stores carry some really tasty readymade options—my favorite is the Jack Daniel's brand. Whichever brand you choose, just remember to pick up a barbecue sauce that complements your pork.

½ pound store-bought or home-made pizza dough, at room temperature

Olive oil cooking spray

Coarse grind cornmeal, for sprinkling

¼ cup barbecue sauce

3 ounces mozzarella, grated (about 1 cup)

3 ounces cheddar, grated (about 1 cup)

1 (16-ounce) package pulled pork with barbecue sauce (about 1½ cups)

1 medium mango, peeled and thinly sliced

½ small red onion, thinly sliced (about ½ cup)

♦ Soak the plank for at least 1 hour and up to 24 hours.

♦ On a well-floured surface, roll out the pizza dough as thinly as possible into a rectangle slightly larger than the plank you are using.

♦ Prepare the plank for grilling according to the instructions on page 12. Lightly spray the toasted side of the plank with the cooking spray and dust with cornmeal. Place the pizza dough on the prepared plank, folding up the edges so that the dough is the same size as the plank. Lightly prick the dough all over with a fork. Close the lid and grill for 5 to 7 minutes, or until the pizza dough is lightly browned and crisp.

♦ Open the grill lid and spread the barbecue sauce evenly over the pizza dough, then sprinkle with the mozzarella and cheddar. Spoon the pulled pork over the cheese and top with the mango and onion. Close the lid and grill until the cheese is golden and bubbly, the pork is warmed, and the mango and onion are cooked through, about 5 minutes.

Sherried Linguica, Grape, and Gorgonzola Pizza

PLANK PREFERENCE:
Alder or Maple

MAKES 4 SERVINGS

2 tablespoons plus 1 teaspoon
  extra-virgin olive oil, divided
4 ounces linguica, cut into ¼-inch-
  thick slices
¼ cup dry sherry
2 cloves garlic, minced
½ teaspoon dried oregano
½ teaspoon dried basil
½ teaspoon kosher salt
¼ teaspoon freshly ground black
  pepper
½ pound store-bought or home-
  made pizza dough, at room
  temperature
Olive oil cooking spray
Coarse grind cornmeal, for
  sprinkling
5 ounces fontina, grated (about
  1¾ cups)
2 ounces Gorgonzola, crumbled
  (about ½ cup)
5 ounces seedless red grapes,
  halved lengthwise (about 1 cup)

My friend Tina Campbell is part Portuguese, and she taught me how to make her family's incredibly delicious sherried linguica one day. She served them with toothpicks as a simple appetizer, and I started to make them all the time for parties. I tried them on a pizza one evening, and no surprise, they are simply amazing. Linguica is found in most grocery stores, especially in areas with large Portuguese populations.

◆ Soak the plank for at least 1 hour and up to 24 hours.

◆ Heat 1 teaspoon of the oil in a large skillet over medium-high heat. Add the linguica and cook, turning over once, until browned on both sides, 7 to 8 minutes. Drain the fat from the pan and add the sherry. Cook for another 3 minutes, or until the sherry has evaporated, scraping up any brown bits left in the bottom of pan. Remove from the heat and set aside.

◆ In a small bowl, whisk the remaining 2 tablespoons of oil with the garlic, oregano, basil, salt, and pepper. Set aside.

◆ On a well-floured surface, roll out the pizza dough as thinly as possible into a rectangle slightly larger than the plank you are using.

◆ Prepare the plank for grilling according to the instructions on page 12. Lightly spray the toasted side of the plank with the cooking spray and dust with cornmeal. Place the pizza dough on the prepared plank, folding up the edges so that the dough is the same size as the plank. Lightly prick the dough all over with a fork. Close the lid and grill for 5 to 7 minutes, or until the pizza dough is lightly browned and crisp.

◆ Open the grill lid and brush the oil mixture evenly over the pizza dough. Sprinkle with the fontina and Gorgonzola, then top with the grapes and linguica. Close the lid and grill until the cheese is golden and bubbly and the grapes are cooked through, about 5 minutes.

Grilled Shrimp, Artichoke, and Pesto Pizza

MAKES 4 SERVINGS

For the pesto:

1½ cups packed fresh basil leaves

1 clove garlic, minced

2 tablespoons toasted pine nuts

Juice of ½ medium lemon (about 1½ tablespoons)

¼ teaspoon kosher salt

¼ teaspoon freshly ground black pepper

¼ cup extra-virgin olive oil

¼ cup freshly grated Parmesan

. . . .

½ pound store-bought or home-made pizza dough, at room temperature

½ pound large shrimp, peeled and deveined, tails removed, and sliced in half lengthwise

¼ teaspoon kosher salt

¼ teaspoon freshly ground black pepper

Olive oil cooking spray

Coarse grind cornmeal, for sprinkling

6 ounces mozzarella, grated (about 2 cups)

Artichokes are one of the few vegetables that taste just as delicious frozen, or even out of a can. Just make sure you don't use jarred marinated artichoke hearts for this recipe; the marinade will compete with the flavors from the pesto and make the pizza crust soggy. Please note that you'll need four skewers for this recipe. Either wooden or metal skewers will work, but if you use wooden ones, be sure to soak them for 30 minutes before grilling so that they don't catch fire.

◆ Soak the plank for at least 1 hour and up to 24 hours.

◆ To make the pesto, combine the basil, garlic, pine nuts, lemon juice, salt, and pepper in the bowl of a food processor and blend for 10 seconds, or until coarsely chopped. With the food processor running, slowly add the oil in a steady stream. Scrape down the sides of the bowl with a spatula, add the Parmesan, and pulse a few more times until well blended. Divide the pesto between 2 medium bowls.

◆ On a well-floured surface, roll out the pizza dough as thinly as possible into a rectangle slightly larger than the plank you are using.

◆ Season the shrimp with the salt and pepper and thread them onto 4 skewers. Place on the barbecue and grill for 1 minute per side. Remove the shrimp from the grill and toss them with the pesto in one of the bowls.

◆ Prepare the plank for grilling according to the instructions on page 12. Lightly spray the toasted side of the plank with the cooking spray and dust with cornmeal. Place the pizza dough on the prepared plank, folding up the edges so that the dough is the same size as the plank. Lightly prick the dough all over with a fork. Close the lid and grill for 5 to 7 minutes, or until the pizza dough is lightly browned and crisp.

◆ Open the grill lid and spread the pesto from the second bowl evenly over the pizza dough, then sprinkle with the mozzarella. Spoon the grilled shrimp over the cheese and top with the artichokes, onion, and feta. Close the lid and grill until the cheese is golden and bubbly and the toppings are cooked through, about 5 minutes.

¾ cup frozen or canned whole artichoke hearts, thawed or drained and roughly chopped
½ small red onion, thinly sliced (about ½ cup)
2 ounces feta, crumbled (about ½ cup)

Roasted Acorn Squash, Caramelized Onion, and Goat Cheese Pizza

Sweet roasted acorn squash tossed with maple syrup tastes spectacular with the flavors of wood and smoke. Peeling acorn squash can be challenging since the sides are not straight and uniform. An easy way to do this is to cut the squash in half, scoop out the seeds, and microwave the squash, cut side up, for one minute. This will slightly tenderize the skin without cooking the flesh. Cut the squash into rings, lay them flat on a cutting board, and cut off the skin. Butternut squash or pumpkin are perfect substitutes for the acorn squash if you can't find it at your local market.

♦ Soak the plank for at least 1 hour and up to 24 hours.

♦ Preheat the oven to 375 degrees F. Line a baking sheet with foil.

♦ In a large bowl, mix 1 tablespoon of the oil with the syrup, caraway seeds, thyme, red pepper flakes, ½ teaspoon of the salt, and ½ teaspoon of the pepper. Add the squash and toss to coat. Place the squash on the prepared baking sheet and bake until tender, 20 to 25 minutes. Set aside.

♦ Meanwhile, heat the remaining 2 tablespoons of oil in a large skillet over medium-high heat. Add the onion, thyme sprigs, garlic, and the remaining ½ teaspoon each of salt and pepper. Reduce the heat to medium and sauté, stirring often, until the onions are soft and golden brown, about 20 minutes. Discard the thyme sprigs. Set aside.

continued

PLANK PREFERENCE:
Alder or Maple

MAKES 4 SERVINGS

3 tablespoons extra-virgin olive oil, divided

2 tablespoons maple syrup

1 teaspoon caraway seeds

1 teaspoon chopped fresh thyme

¼ teaspoon crushed red pepper flakes

1 teaspoon kosher salt, divided

1 teaspoon freshly ground black pepper, divided

1 small acorn squash (about 1 pound), peeled, seeded, and cut into ½-inch dice

1 large onion (about 1 pound), halved and thinly sliced

2 thyme sprigs

1 garlic clove, thinly sliced

½ pound store-bought or home-made pizza dough, at room temperature

Olive oil cooking spray

Coarse grind cornmeal, for
sprinkling

6 ounces fontina, grated (about
2 cups)

2 ounces goat cheese, crumbled
(about ½ cup)

4 large fresh basil leaves, sliced
chiffonade (see note, page 43)

◆ On a well-floured surface, roll out the pizza dough as thinly as possible into a rectangle slightly larger than the plank you are using.

◆ Prepare the plank for grilling according to the instructions on page 12. Lightly spray the toasted side of the plank with the cooking spray and dust with cornmeal. Place the pizza dough on the prepared plank, folding up the edges so that the dough is the same size as the plank. Lightly prick the dough all over with a fork. Close the lid and grill for 5 to 7 minutes, or until the pizza dough is lightly browned and crisp.

◆ Open the grill lid and spread the caramelized onions over the pizza dough. Sprinkle with the fontina and top with a thin layer of roasted squash (there may be some leftover) and a layer of goat cheese. Close the lid and grill until the cheese is golden and bubbly, about 5 minutes. Transfer the pizza to a clean work surface and sprinkle with the basil.

Pizza with Potatoes, Caramelized Onions, Pancetta, and Goat Cheese

Yes, potatoes on a pizza. I tried my first potato-topped pizza at One Stop, one of my favorite restaurants in Sacramento, and I've been hooked ever since. I wanted to try and recreate it for this book, and plank-grilling the pizza takes it to another level altogether. Infused with a little bit of smoke, the potatoes give this pizza a rich complexity, pairing perfectly with the Mediterranean flavors of kalamata olives and goat cheese.

* Soak the plank for at least 1 hour and up to 24 hours.

* Preheat the oven to 425 degrees F.

* In a medium bowl, toss the potatoes with 1 tablespoon of the oil until coated. Season with ¼ teaspoon each of the salt and pepper. Spread the potatoes in a single layer on a baking sheet and roast until golden and tender, 20 to 22 minutes.

* Heat the remaining 1 tablespoon of oil in a large skillet over medium-high heat. Add the pancetta and cook until brown, 7 to 8 minutes. Using a slotted spoon, transfer the pancetta to a small bowl.

* Add the onion, thyme sprigs, garlic, and the remaining ¼ teaspoon each of salt and pepper to the skillet. Reduce the heat to medium and sauté, stirring occasionally, until the onions are soft and deep golden brown, about 20 minutes. Discard the thyme sprigs. Set aside.

continued

PLANK PREFERENCE:
Alder or Maple

MAKES 4 SERVINGS

3 small Yukon Gold or red potatoes (about 10 ounces), cut into ¼-inch-thick rounds

2 tablespoons extra-virgin olive oil, divided

½ teaspoon kosher salt, divided

½ teaspoon freshly ground black pepper, divided

4 ounces pancetta, cut into ¼-inch dice (about ¾ cup)

1 large onion (about 1 pound), halved and thinly sliced

2 thyme sprigs

1 garlic clove, thinly sliced

½ pound store-bought or homemade pizza dough, at room temperature

Olive oil cooking spray

Coarse grind cornmeal, for sprinkling

5 ounces mozzarella, grated (about 1¾ cups)

½ cup sliced kalamata olives

2 ounces goat cheese, crumbled (about ½ cup)

◆ On a well-floured surface, roll out the pizza dough as thinly as possible into a rectangle slightly larger than the plank you are using.

◆ Prepare the plank for grilling according to the instructions on page 12. Lightly spray the toasted side of the plank with the cooking spray and dust with cornmeal. Place the pizza dough on the prepared plank, folding up the edges so that the dough is the same size as the plank. Lightly prick the dough all over with a fork. Close the lid and grill for 5 to 7 minutes, or until the pizza dough is lightly browned and crisp.

◆ Open the grill lid and spread the caramelized onions over the pizza dough, then sprinkle with the mozzarella. Top with the potatoes, pancetta, olives, and goat cheese. Close the lid and grill until the cheese is golden and bubbly and the toppings are warmed through, about 5 minutes.

Corn, Chorizo, and Poblano Pizza

Poblano chiles are fresh green chiles. They vary in spiciness, so the best way to test a poblano's heat level is by tasting it. The Mexican chorizo called for in this recipe is not the same as Spanish chorizo. Mexican chorizo usually comes wrapped in thin plastic and falls apart like ground beef when cooked.

PLANK PREFERENCE:
Alder or Maple

MAKES 4 SERVINGS

- ◆ Soak the plank for at least 1 hour and up to 24 hours.

- ◆ Line a large plate with paper towels. Cook the chorizo in a large skillet over medium-high heat, crumbling with the back of a spoon, until browned, about 10 minutes. Using a slotted spoon, transfer the chorizo to the lined plate to drain.

- ◆ On a well-floured surface, roll out the pizza dough as thinly as possible into a rectangle slightly larger than the plank you are using.

- ◆ Prepare the plank for grilling according to the instructions on page 12. Lightly spray the toasted side of the plank with the cooking spray and dust with cornmeal. Place the pizza dough on the prepared plank, folding up the edges so that the dough is the same size as the plank. Lightly prick the dough all over with a fork. Close the lid and grill for 5 to 7 minutes, or until the pizza dough is lightly browned and crisp.

- ◆ Open the grill lid and sprinkle the pizza dough with the mozzarella and Monterey Jack. Top with the chorizo, corn, onion, poblano, and queso fresco. Close the lid and grill until the cheese is golden and bubbly and the vegetables are cooked through, about 5 minutes. Transfer the pizza to a clean work surface and sprinkle with the cilantro and green onions.

10 ounces Mexican chorizo, casings removed

½ pound store-bought or home-made pizza dough, at room temperature

Olive oil cooking spray

Coarse grind cornmeal, for sprinkling

3 ounces mozzarella, grated (about 1 cup)

3 ounces Monterey Jack, grated (about 1 cup)

¾ cup fresh or frozen corn, thawed if frozen

½ small red onion, thinly sliced (about ½ cup)

1 poblano chile, seeded and cut into ¼-inch dice

2 ounces queso fresco, crumbled (about ½ cup)

2 tablespoons chopped fresh cilantro

2 green onions, thinly sliced

NOTE: You can find poblanos, Mexican chorizo, and queso fresco at Latin American markets and many supermarkets. If you can't find queso fresco, feta cheese makes a good substitute.

Caramel Apple Pizza

One of my favorite desserts to plank-grill is apples stuffed with nuts and sugar and drizzled with caramel. In this version, you get the added luscious satisfaction of melted chocolate and a crispy, chewy crust. When grilling this pizza, be sure to check it 2 minutes after adding the toppings because the chocolate and nuts can burn very quickly.

PLANK PREFERENCE:
Alder or Maple

MAKES 4 SERVINGS

2 tablespoons unsalted butter
2 Granny Smith apples (about
    1 pound), peeled, cored, sliced
    ¼ inch thick, and tossed with
    1 tablespoon freshly squeezed
    lemon juice
¼ cup packed brown sugar
½ teaspoon ground cinnamon
½ pound store-bought or home-
    made pizza dough, at room
    temperature
Olive oil cooking spray
Coarse grind cornmeal, for
    sprinkling
1½ ounces semisweet chocolate,
    coarsely chopped (about
    ¼ cup)
¼ cup sliced almonds
2 tablespoons caramel sauce

◆ Soak the plank for at least 1 hour and up to 24 hours.

◆ Melt the butter in a large skillet over medium-high heat. Add the apples, brown sugar, and cinnamon and sauté, stirring occasionally, until the apples are tender, 7 to 10 minutes.

◆ On a well-floured surface, roll out the pizza dough as thinly as possible into a rectangle slightly larger than the plank you are using.

◆ Prepare the plank for grilling according to the instructions on page 12. Lightly spray the toasted side of the plank with the cooking spray and dust with cornmeal. Place the pizza dough on the prepared plank, folding up the edges so that the dough is the same size as the plank. Lightly prick the dough all over with a fork. Close the lid and grill for 5 to 7 minutes, or until the pizza dough is lightly browned and crisp.

◆ Open the grill lid and, using a slotted spoon, spread the apple mixture over the pizza dough, leaving behind any juices so that the crust does not become soggy. Sprinkle with the chocolate and almonds. Close the lid and grill until the chocolate has melted, about 2 minutes. Transfer the pizza to a clean work surface and let cool for 10 minutes. Drizzle with the caramel sauce before serving.

S'mores Pizza

PLANK PREFERENCE:
Alder or Maple

MAKES 4 SERVINGS

½ cup graham cracker crumbs
(from 8 graham cracker squares
ground in a food processor)
2 tablespoons unsalted butter,
melted
½ pound store-bought or home-
made pizza dough, at room
temperature
Olive oil cooking spray
Coarse grind cornmeal, for
sprinkling
1 cup miniature marshmallows
3 ounces semisweet chocolate,
coarsely chopped (about
½ cup)
¼ cup sliced almonds (optional)

Munching on this pizza makes me happy. It's not just the flavors of the melted chocolate and gooey, golden marsh-mallows. It's because even as I sit in my backyard hearing the traffic whiz by, I feel like I'm camping in the forests of Tahoe, where my family spends a lot of time in the summers. The smell of the wood smoking and the flavors of this pizza might have the same effect on you. It's cathartic. Just don't Zen out too quickly because marshmallows and chocolate burn easily—be sure to check the pizza after a few minutes of grilling.

◆ Soak the plank for at least 1 hour and up to 24 hours.

◆ In a medium bowl, combine the graham cracker crumbs and melted butter. Set aside.

◆ On a well-floured surface, roll out the pizza dough as thinly as possible into a rectangle slightly larger than the plank you are using.

◆ Prepare the plank for grilling according to the instructions on page 12. Lightly spray the toasted side of the plank with the cooking spray and dust with cornmeal. Place the pizza dough on the prepared plank, folding up the edges so that the dough is the same size as the plank. Lightly prick the dough all over with a fork. Close the lid and grill for 5 to 7 minutes, or until the pizza dough is lightly browned and crisp.

◆ Open the grill lid and sprinkle the marshmallows, chocolate, graham cracker mixture, and almonds over the pizza dough. Close the lid and grill until the choco-late has just melted and the marshmallows are golden, about 2 minutes. Transfer the pizza to a clean work sur-face and let cool for 5 minutes before serving.

Peach Cobbler Pizza

PLANK PREFERENCE:
Alder or Maple

MAKES 4 SERVINGS

2 tablespoons unsalted butter

2 ripe peaches (about ¾ pound), pitted and cut into ¼-inch-thick slices

¼ cup packed brown sugar

½ teaspoon ground cinnamon

½ pound store-bought or home-made pizza dough, at room temperature

Olive oil cooking spray

Coarse grind cornmeal, for sprinkling

½ cup granola

2 tablespoons caramel sauce

Warm plank-grilled peaches served with vanilla ice cream are nothing short of amazing. So I knew that this pizza would be a hit. In place of the vanilla ice cream, my husband, Roland, suggested granola. It has the perfect sweetness and consistency, giving this pizza a nice crunch, and it soaks up the smoke flavor beautifully.

◆ Soak the plank for at least 1 hour and up to 24 hours.

◆ Melt the butter in a large skillet over medium heat. Add the peaches, brown sugar, and cinnamon and cook, stirring often, until the sugar has dissolved and the peaches are warmed through, 3 to 5 minutes.

◆ On a well-floured surface, roll out the pizza dough as thinly as possible into a rectangle slightly larger than the plank you are using.

◆ Prepare the plank for grilling according to the instructions on page 12. Lightly spray the toasted side of the plank with the cooking spray and dust with cornmeal. Place the pizza dough on the prepared plank, folding up the edges so that the dough is the same size as the plank. Lightly prick the dough all over with a fork. Close the lid and grill for 5 to 7 minutes, or until the pizza dough is lightly browned and crisp.

◆ Open the grill lid and, using a slotted spoon, spread the peach mixture over the pizza dough, leaving behind any juices so that the crust does not become soggy. Sprinkle with the granola. Close the lid and grill until the peaches are warmed through, about 2 minutes. Transfer the pizza to a clean work surface and let cool for 10 minutes. Drizzle with the caramel sauce before serving.

SEAFOOD

Spice-Rubbed Salmon with
Blackberry Ginger Glaze 71

Salmon with Sherry Tomato
Sauce 73

Fig-and-Fennel-Glazed Salmon 74

Salmon Glazed with
Orange and Miso 76

Salmon with Cantaloupe
Lemongrass Sauce 77

Bacon-Wrapped
Shrimp Teriyaki 78

Asian Shrimp in Lettuce Wraps 79

Whole Fish Stuffed with Fennel
and Orange 80

Tortilla-Crusted Tilapia with Papaya
Peach Salsa 82

Coconut-Crusted Mahi Mahi with
Mango Basil Salsa 83

Halibut Wrapped in Grape Leaves
with Lemon Caper Sauce 86

Trout Pâté 88

his is the chapter you will probably come to over and over again because no matter how versatile the plank is with pork and chicken and vegetables and pizza, there is nothing like cedar plank–grilled salmon.

Salmon has a stronger flavor than other kinds of seafood, making it pair best with the spicy, sweet smokiness of cedar wood, as well as the vanilla and nutty smokiness of alder wood. It pairs so well with these woods that all you need to do is sprinkle salmon with salt and pepper, grill it on a cedar or alder plank, and let the wood and smoke work their magic. But if you want to try something truly spectacular, prepare a sauce from the following pages and spread it on the salmon just before grilling.

In addition to salmon, this chapter also focuses on the milder flavors of white fish and shrimp. While cedar is a popular choice for these ingredients too, here's your chance to experiment with other woods to discover how they can change the flavor of a dish. The lighter, more buttery maple wood or the vanilla and nutty smokiness of alder are perfect options.

Spice-Rubbed Salmon with Blackberry Ginger Glaze

I love making my own spice rubs. They are always healthier than store-bought versions since I use a lot less salt and don't add preservatives and chemicals like monosodium glutamate, which many of my friends and family members are allergic to. This spice rub gives salmon the perfect kick and works so well with the sweetness of the Blackberry Ginger Glaze. The glaze can be made ahead and stored for up to 3 days in the refrigerator.

• Soak the plank for at least 1 hour and up to 24 hours.

• In a small bowl, combine the coriander, cumin, salt, and cayenne. Rub the spice mixture all over the salmon and let it rest at room temperature for 30 minutes.

• Meanwhile, prepare the glaze. Combine the blackberries, water, sugar, balsamic vinegar, ginger, salt, and pepper in the bowl of a food processor and puree until smooth. Pour the mixture through a fine-mesh sieve into a small saucepan, discarding the solids left behind. Bring to a boil over medium-high heat and simmer, stirring occasionally, for 12 to 15 minutes, or until the glaze becomes thick and syrupy and is reduced to about ½ cup. Remove the pan from the heat and let the glaze cool to room temperature.

• Prepare the plank for grilling according to the instructions on page 12. Place the salmon on the toasted side of the plank. Brush the glaze evenly over the salmon. Close the lid and grill for 10 to 15 minutes, or until the salmon flakes easily with a fork.

PLANK PREFERENCE: Cedar

MAKES 4 SERVINGS

½ teaspoon ground coriander
¼ teaspoon ground cumin
¼ teaspoon kosher salt
⅛ teaspoon cayenne pepper
1 (1½ pound) skinless salmon fillet

For the glaze:
6 ounces blackberries (about 1½ cups)
½ cup water
¼ cup sugar
2 tablespoons balsamic vinegar
1 tablespoon freshly grated ginger
½ teaspoon kosher salt
¼ teaspoon freshly ground black pepper

Salmon with Sherry Tomato Sauce

If you're a foodie, there are dishes you've had in your life that never leave you, and in some cases, inspire you. In my senior year of high school, I was required to take an independent-study course in a subject of my choosing. I chose a culinary program where I had the chance to try the most delicious sherried tomato soup, and I never forgot how wonderful the flavors were together. Several years later (no need to discuss how many, exactly) those flavors motivated me to create this dish. A side of rice and a light green salad are perfect accompaniments.

• Soak the plank for at least 1 hour and up to 24 hours.

• Heat the oil in a saucepan over medium-high heat. Add the shallot, ½ teaspoon of the salt, and ¼ teaspoon of the pepper and cook, stirring often, until softened, 3 to 5 minutes. Add the sherry and chicken stock and bring to a boil. Cook until the sauce is reduced to ½ cup, about 10 minutes. Add the tomatoes, vinegar, and tarragon and stir to combine. Remove the pan from the heat and let the sauce cool to room temperature.

• Prepare the plank for grilling according to the instructions on page 12. Season the salmon with the remaining ¼ teaspoon each of salt and pepper. Place the salmon on the toasted side of the plank. Spoon the sauce evenly over the salmon and close the lid. Grill for 10 to 15 minutes, or until the salmon flakes easily with a fork.

PLANK PREFERENCE: Cedar

MAKES 4 SERVINGS

1 tablespoon extra-virgin olive oil
1 shallot, finely chopped
¾ teaspoon kosher salt, divided
½ teaspoon freshly ground black pepper, divided
½ cup dry sherry
½ cup low-sodium chicken stock
9 ounces cherry tomatoes, quartered (about 2 cups)
1 tablespoon sherry vinegar
1 tablespoon chopped fresh tarragon
1 (1½ pound) skinless salmon fillet

Fig-and-Fennel-Glazed Salmon

PLANK PREFERENCE: Cedar

MAKES 4 SERVINGS

1 tablespoon extra-virgin olive oil

1 small fennel bulb (about
½ pound), thinly sliced

¾ teaspoon kosher salt, divided

¾ teaspoon freshly ground black
pepper, divided

¼ cup fig jam

2 tablespoons packed brown
sugar

2 teaspoons Dijon mustard

2 teaspoons balsamic vinegar

1 clove garlic, minced

1 (1½ pound) skinless salmon fillet

2 teaspoons roughly chopped
fennel fronds

This is a very flavorful planked salmon dish with caramelized fennel, fig jam, Dijon mustard, and balsamic vinegar, so you'll want something restrained to accompany it, like potatoes or rice. If you can't find fig jam, you can substitute blackberry, raspberry, or cherry preserves. The glaze can be made ahead and stored for up to 3 days in the refrigerator.

◆ Soak the plank for at least 1 hour and up to 24 hours.

◆ In a large skillet, heat the oil over medium-high heat. Add the fennel, ½ teaspoon of the salt, and ½ teaspoon of the pepper and sauté, stirring occasionally, until softened and lightly caramelized, 7 to 8 minutes. Add the fig jam, brown sugar, mustard, balsamic vinegar, and garlic. Stir to combine and cook for an additional 30 seconds, or until the glaze thickens slightly. Remove the pan from the heat and let the glaze cool to room temperature.

◆ Prepare the plank for grilling according to the instructions on page 12. Season the salmon with the remaining ¼ teaspoon each of salt and pepper. Place the salmon on the toasted side of the plank. Use a spatula to spread the glaze evenly over the salmon. Close the lid and grill for 10 to 15 minutes, or until the salmon flakes easily with a fork. Sprinkle with the chopped fennel fronds.

Salmon Glazed with Orange and Miso

PLANK PREFERENCE: Cedar

MAKES 4 SERVINGS

2 tablespoons white miso
2 tablespoons orange marmalade
1 teaspoon mirin
1 teaspoon low-sodium soy sauce
1 clove garlic, minced
1 teaspoon freshly grated ginger
1 (1½ pound) skinless salmon fillet
¼ cup finely sliced green onions
1 tablespoon toasted sesame
   seeds

. . . .

NOTE: White miso, a Japanese fermented paste often made out of soybeans, can be found in the refrigerated section of your grocery store, usually next to the tofu. Mirin is a Japanese sweet rice wine that can be found in the Asian section of your grocery store or in any Asian market.

This salmon dish is so irresistible that it has made it into my friend Kristin Ross's birthday menu rotation. When someone in her family has a birthday, they choose their favorite foods to be served for their dinner, and Kristin's daughter Emily has requested this salmon. What an honor, and I'd like to take all the credit, but the truth is that Asian flavors pair exceptionally well with the wood and smoke infusion you get from plank grilling.

◆ Soak the plank for at least 1 hour and up to 24 hours.

◆ In a small bowl, whisk the miso, marmalade, mirin, soy sauce, garlic, and ginger until combined.

◆ Prepare the plank for grilling according to the instructions on page 12. Place the salmon on the toasted side of the plank. Brush the glaze evenly over the salmon. Close the lid and grill for 10 to 15 minutes, or until the salmon flakes easily with a fork. Sprinkle with the green onions and sesame seeds.

Salmon with Cantaloupe Lemongrass Sauce

I know this sounds like a strange combination—salmon, cantaloupe, and lemongrass—but it has incredible flavors that are truly harmonious together. The sweetness and complexity of the sauce combined with the spicy cedar wood, delicious salmon, and aromatic smoke produces a wonderfully rich dish. My friend Betsy Black tested all the salmon recipes in this book and concluded that this one was her favorite.

PLANK PREFERENCE: Cedar

MAKES 4 SERVINGS

2 tablespoons extra-virgin olive oil

1 thick stalk lemongrass, white part only, finely minced (about 2½ tablespoons)

1 cantaloupe, cut into ½-inch dice (about 3 cups)

¼ cup honey

¼ cup unseasoned rice vinegar

2 cloves garlic, minced

1 teaspoon freshly grated ginger

¼ teaspoon crushed red pepper flakes

1 teaspoon kosher salt, divided

½ teaspoon freshly ground black pepper

¼ cup roughly chopped fresh cilantro, plus more for garnish

1 (1½ pound) skinless salmon fillet

• Soak the plank for at least 1 hour and up to 24 hours.

• Heat the oil in a saucepan over medium-low heat. Add the lemongrass and cook, stirring occasionally, for 5 minutes, or until softened. Add the cantaloupe, honey, vinegar, garlic, ginger, red pepper flakes, ½ teaspoon of the salt, and ¼ teaspoon of the pepper and stir to combine. Raise the heat to medium-high, bring to a boil, and simmer for 20 to 25 minutes, or until slightly thickened. Remove the sauce from the heat, stir in the cilantro, and let cool to room temperature.

• Prepare the plank for grilling according to the instructions on page 12. Season the salmon with the remaining ½ teaspoon of salt and ¼ teaspoon of pepper. Place the salmon on the toasted side of the plank. Spoon the sauce evenly over the salmon. Close the lid and grill for 10 to 15 minutes, or until the salmon flakes easily with a fork. Sprinkle with additional cilantro.

Bacon-Wrapped Shrimp Teriyaki

MAKES 6 TO 8 SERVINGS

For the sauce:

1 tablespoon mirin

½ teaspoon cornstarch

¼ cup low-sodium soy sauce

¼ cup sugar

1 teaspoon freshly grated ginger

1 teaspoon minced garlic

. . . .

16 jumbo shrimp

¼ teaspoon Chinese five-spice
powder

16 (¾-inch) cubes fresh or canned
pineapple

8 thick slices pepper bacon, cut
in half

16 wooden toothpicks

. . . .

NOTE: Mirin is a Japanese sweet
rice wine that can be found in the
Asian section of your grocery store
or in any Asian market, as can Chinese five-spice powder.

These shrimp are a prime example of the benefits of plank
grilling. Bacon-wrapped shrimp is a classic appetizer that
has been on many restaurant menus and home kitchen
tables, but plank grilling adds a depth of flavor you can't get
from broiling in the oven. Grilling shrimp on your barbecue
is an inconvenience when you spend most of your time trying to keep the shrimp from falling in between the grates,
but plank grilling alleviates that hassle since you can simply
toss them on the cedar plank. It just doesn't get any easier
or taste any better—adding pineapple and teriyaki sauce is
just showing off.

◆ Soak the plank for at least 1 hour and up to 24 hours.

◆ To prepare the sauce, in a small bowl, combine the mirin
and cornstarch and stir until smooth. In a small saucepan,
combine the soy sauce, sugar, ginger, and garlic and bring
to a boil over medium-high heat. Stir in the mirin mixture
and cook until slightly thickened, about 1 minute. Remove
the sauce from the heat. Set aside.

◆ In a medium bowl, toss the shrimp with the Chinese
five-spice powder. Nestle a pineapple chunk in the curve
of each shrimp, wrap with a piece of bacon, and secure
with a toothpick. Repeat with the remaining shrimp.

◆ Prepare the plank for grilling according to the instructions on page 12. Place the shrimp on the toasted side of
the plank. Close the lid and grill for 15 to 20 minutes, or
until the bacon is crisp. Drizzle with the sauce.

Asian Shrimp in Lettuce Wraps

For a quick and delicious dinner, making these wraps doesn't get any easier. The shrimp can be substituted for fish, chicken, or pork. Assembling the wraps with a few sprigs of cilantro and toasted sesame seeds takes this dish over the top.

PLANK PREFERENCE: Cedar, Alder, Maple, or Cherry

MAKES 4 SERVINGS

- Soak the plank for at least 1 hour and up to 24 hours.

- In a large, nonreactive bowl, combine the plum sauce, soy sauce, sesame oil, garlic, ginger, and red pepper flakes and whisk well. Add the shrimp and toss to coat. Marinate in the refrigerator for 30 minutes.

- Prepare the plank for grilling according to the instructions on page 12. Place the shrimp on the toasted side of the plank in a single layer; it is important not to let them overlap. (If the shrimp do not fit in a single layer, then grill them in batches.) Close the lid and grill for 5 minutes, or until the shrimp have turned pink. Be careful not to overcook the shrimp, as they will become chewy.

- To serve, place 2 to 3 shrimp, a few cilantro sprigs, a sprinkle of sesame seeds, and a drizzle of additional plum sauce on each lettuce leaf and wrap.

1¼ cups plum sauce, plus more for serving
¼ cup soy sauce
1 tablespoon sesame oil
1 teaspoon minced garlic
1 teaspoon freshly grated ginger
½ teaspoon crushed red pepper flakes
24 jumbo shrimp (about 2 pounds), peeled and deveined
1 cup cilantro sprigs
2 tablespoons toasted sesame seeds
Bibb lettuce, for wrapping

Whole Fish Stuffed with Fennel and Orange

PLANK PREFERENCE: Cedar

MAKES 2 TO 4 SERVINGS

1 small fennel bulb (about
   ½ pound), thinly sliced
¼ cup plus 2 tablespoons roughly
   chopped fennel fronds, divided
½ medium orange, cut into 6 thin
   slices
1 tablespoon chopped fresh
   rosemary
1½ teaspoons kosher salt, divided
¾ teaspoon freshly ground black
   pepper, divided
2 (1½-pound) whole fish, cleaned

For the sauce:
¼ cup unsalted butter, cut into
   4 pieces
Juice from ½ orange (about
   ¼ cup)
1 tablespoon low-sodium soy
   sauce

I grew up eating fish served whole with head and tail intact, but I know that doesn't appeal to everyone. If that's the case, just ask your fishmonger to remove the head and tail before you bring the fish home. Practically any whole fish will work for this dish: branzino, snapper, and sea bass are some of my favorites.

◆ Soak the plank for at least 1 hour and up to 24 hours.

◆ In a large bowl, toss together the fennel, ¼ cup of the chopped fennel fronds, orange, rosemary, ½ teaspoon of the salt, and ¼ teaspoon of the pepper until combined. Sprinkle the fish inside and out with the remaining 1 teaspoon of salt and ½ teaspoon of pepper. Stuff each fish with half of the fennel mixture.

◆ Prepare the plank for grilling according to the instructions on page 12. Place the stuffed fish on the toasted side of the plank. Close the lid and grill for 15 minutes, or until the fish is opaque and flakes easily with a fork. Transfer to a serving platter.

◆ To prepare the sauce, in a small skillet, melt the butter over medium heat. Once the butter has melted, slowly swirl the pan as the solids begin to turn brown and smell nutty. This happens in just minutes and can quickly burn, so keep your eye on it the whole time. Making sure the pan is still over medium heat (any hotter and it will splatter when liquids are added), add the orange juice and soy sauce and whisk until combined, about 30 seconds. Pour the sauce over the fish, sprinkle with the remaining 2 tablespoons of fennel fronds, and serve immediately.

Tortilla-Crusted Tilapia with Papaya Peach Salsa

PLANK PREFERENCE:
Cedar, Alder, or Maple

MAKES 4 SERVINGS

This recipe could really be called "Tortilla Crusted Fish" because this crust works on almost any fish fillets that are at least ¼ inch thick, so don't feel like you need to use tilapia. And if you're not a big fan of papaya, try other tropical fruits like pineapple or mango—they'll work just as well. Be sure to zest your lime for the crust before juicing it for the salsa.

For the salsa:
1½ cups diced papaya
1½ cups diced peaches
½ cup diced red onion
⅓ cup chopped fresh cilantro
½ jalapeño, seeded and minced
Juice of 1 large lime (about
    2 tablespoons)
½ teaspoon kosher salt
¼ teaspoon freshly ground black
    pepper
¼ teaspoon chili powder

. . . .

3 ounces tortilla chips
¼ cup roughly chopped fresh
    cilantro
½ jalapeño, seeded and roughly
    chopped
Zest of 1 large lime (about
    2 teaspoons)
2 tablespoons Dijon mustard
¼ teaspoon chili powder
¼ teaspoon ground cumin
¼ teaspoon ground coriander
4 (6-ounce) tilapia fillets
½ teaspoon kosher salt
¼ teaspoon freshly ground black
    pepper
Lime wedges, for garnish

◆ Soak the plank for at least 1 hour and up to 24 hours.

◆ To prepare the salsa, in a large bowl, combine the papaya, peaches, onion, cilantro, jalapeño, lime juice, salt, pepper, and chili powder. The salsa can be prepared and refrigerated up to 2 hours in advance.

◆ Put the tortilla chips, cilantro, jalapeño, and lime zest in a food processor and pulse until the chips are reduced to small crumbs and the mixture is completely combined. Spread the crumb mixture in a pie plate.

◆ In a small bowl, stir the mustard, chili powder, cumin, and coriander until combined.

◆ Season the tilapia with the salt and pepper. Brush the top of each fillet with the mustard mixture, then press them, mustard side down, into the crumb mixture. Pat the tilapia lightly to make sure the crumbs adhere.

◆ Prepare the plank for grilling according to the instructions on page 12. Place the tilapia on the toasted side of the plank, tortilla-crusted side up. Close the lid and grill for 10 minutes, or until the tilapia flakes easily with a fork. Serve with the salsa and lime wedges.

Coconut-Crusted Mahi Mahi with Mango Basil Salsa

As you look over the ingredient list for this recipe, you will notice that only 2 tablespoons of coconut milk are required, after which you will probably curse every cookbook author who asks you to go buy a full can or jar of something when you only need a smidgen of it. My cousin Odette was testing this recipe when the same thing happened to her (cursing me included, I'm sure). She came up with the brilliant idea of using the left-over coconut milk to make coconut rice as an accompaniment to the fish (see sidebar, page 85, for a quick recipe). Combined with the Mango Basil Salsa, the coconut rice makes this a really fabulous meal. If you still don't want to purchase the coconut milk, however, regular milk is a fine substitute.

• Soak the plank for at least 1 hour and up to 24 hours.

• In a small bowl, combine the salt, coriander, and cayenne.

• Set up an assembly line of 3 pie plates. In the first pie plate, combine the flour with 1 teaspoon of the seasoning mixture. In the second pie plate, whisk the egg, coconut milk, and ½ teaspoon of the seasoning mixture. In the third pie plate, combine the coconut, panko, and 1 teaspoon of the seasoning mixture.

• Season the mahi mahi with the remaining ¾ teaspoon of seasoning mixture. Dredge a fillet in the flour mixture, patting off any excess, then dip it in the egg mixture. Finally dredge it in the coconut mixture, pressing lightly to coat, and transfer to a large plate. Repeat with the remaining fillets.

continued

MAKES 4 SERVINGS

2 teaspoons kosher salt

1 teaspoon ground coriander

¼ teaspoon cayenne pepper

½ cup all-purpose flour

1 large egg

2 tablespoons unsweetened coconut milk

1½ cups sweetened flaked coconut

⅓ cup panko

4 (6-ounce) mahi mahi fillets

For the salsa:

2 large ripe mangos, peeled, pitted, and diced

¼ cup chopped red onion

5 large fresh basil leaves, sliced chiffonade (see note, page 43)

Juice of 1 large lime (about 2 tablespoons)

½ teaspoon kosher salt

¼ teaspoon freshly ground black pepper

◆ Let the mahi mahi sit at room temperature while you make the salsa. In a large bowl, combine the mangos, onion, basil, lime juice, salt, and pepper and set aside.

◆ Prepare the plank for grilling according to the instructions on page 12. Place the mahi mahi on the toasted side of the plank. Close the lid and grill for 12 to 15 minutes, or until the mahi mahi is golden brown and flakes easily with a fork. Serve with the salsa and coconut rice, if desired.

Easy Coconut Rice

◆ Rinse the jasmine rice until the water runs clear. Combine the rice, coconut milk, water, and salt in a medium saucepan. Bring to a boil over medium-high heat. Reduce the heat to low, cover tightly, and cook for 15 minutes. Remove the saucepan from the heat and let it sit, covered, for 10 minutes before fluffing with a fork.

MAKES 3 CUPS

1 cup jasmine rice
1 (13.5-ounce) can coconut milk, minus the 2 tablespoons used in the Coconut-Crusted Mahi Mahi (page 83)
1¼ cups water
½ teaspoon kosher salt

Halibut Wrapped in Grape Leaves with Lemon Caper Sauce

PLANK PREFERENCE: Maple

MAKES 4 SERVINGS

For the sauce:
⅓ cup extra-virgin olive oil
Juice of 1 medium lemon (about
    3 tablespoons)
2 tablespoons capers
1 teaspoon chopped fresh thyme
⅛ teaspoon kosher salt
⅛ teaspoon freshly ground black
    pepper

. . . .

1 (1 pound) halibut fillet
Kosher salt and freshly ground
    black pepper
12 brined grape leaves, rinsed
    and stemmed
⅓ cup extra-virgin olive oil
Zest of 2 medium lemons (about
    2 tablespoons)
12 thin slices red onion
1 tablespoon chopped fresh
    flat-leaf parsley
1 tablespoon chopped fresh
    thyme

Grilling grape leaves on a plank gives them the most delicious smoky, caramelized flavor. This recipe works best with maple wood since it has a delicate smokiness that really complements the grape leaves and sauce in this dish. Any firm white fish can be substituted for the halibut, such as red snapper, bass, grouper, or swordfish. If you are using fresh grape leaves, it is important to remove the stems and blanch the leaves in boiling water for 5 minutes before wrapping them around the fish.

◆ Soak the plank for at least 1 hour and up to 24 hours.

◆ To prepare the sauce, in a small bowl, whisk the oil, lemon juice, capers, thyme, salt, and pepper together until well combined. Set aside.

◆ Cut the halibut into 12 pieces and season them with salt and pepper. Lay out the grape leaves on a clean work surface, vein side up (this is the dull side of the grape leaf). Put the oil in a large, shallow dish. Roll a piece of fish in the oil and place it in the center of a grape leaf. Sprinkle with a little of the lemon zest, place an onion slice on top, and scatter a little of the parsley and thyme over it. Fold the sides of the leaf over the fish, fold up the bottom, and roll up the fish neatly. Repeat with the remaining fish. Place the halibut rolls back in the dish with any remaining oil, turning them to make sure all sides are coated.

• Prepare the plank for grilling according to the instructions on page 12. Place the fish rolls, seam side down, on the toasted side of the plank. Close the lid and grill for 10 minutes. Cut into one of the rolls and check for doneness. The fish should be opaque and flake easily with a fork.

• Transfer the rolls to 4 serving plates and pour a little of the sauce over each roll. The remaining sauce can be served on the side. Have guests unwrap the rolls at the table, pour a little more sauce over the fish, and eat the grape leaves with the fish.

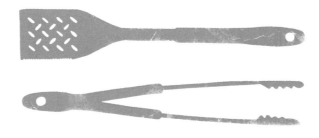

Trout Pâté

PLANK PREFERENCE:
Cedar or Alder

MAKES 2 CUPS

1 (1½-pound) whole rainbow trout, cleaned

1½ teaspoons kosher salt, divided

¾ teaspoon freshly ground black pepper, divided

4 ounces cream cheese, at room temperature

½ cup sour cream

1½ tablespoons snipped fresh dill

Juice of ½ large lemon (about 2 tablespoons)

1 teaspoon prepared horseradish

This pâté is always a favorite at parties. It has the perfect balance of smokiness from the fish, creaminess from the cream cheese, and brightness from the lemon juice. It has the added benefit of being easy to make and incredibly versatile. The whole trout can be substituted by other whole fish like mackerel or haddock, and if you prefer to grill with boneless fillets, salmon makes a delicious option. Just plank-grill ¾ pound skinless salmon fillet instead of the trout and shred it into small pieces before adding it to the food processor with the other ingredients. Serve with crackers, toast points, or sliced cucumbers. The pâté can be made ahead and stored for up to 1 week in the refrigerator.

◆ Soak the plank for at least 1 hour and up to 24 hours.

◆ Season the trout inside and out with 1 teaspoon of the salt and ½ teaspoon of the pepper.

◆ Prepare the plank for grilling according to the instructions on page 12. Place the trout on the toasted side of the plank. Close the lid and grill for 15 minutes, or until the trout flakes easily with a fork. Let the trout cool to room temperature, then use your hands to shred it into small pieces, discarding the skin and bones.

◆ Place the trout, cream cheese, sour cream, dill, lemon juice, horseradish, and the remaining ½ teaspoon of salt and ¼ teaspoon of pepper in a food processor and blend until the pâté is smooth and spreadable. Chill for at least 2 hours before serving.

PORK & POULTRY

Homemade Bacon 91

Homemade Tasso 93

Orange-Balsamic-Glazed Pork
Chops Stuffed with Sweet Potatoes
and Chorizo 95

Pork Chops Stuffed with Couscous,
Peaches, and Bacon 98

Pork Loin with Dried Plums and
Soy Caramel Sauce 100

Pork Tenderloin with Raspberry
Chipotle Sauce 102

Spare Ribs with Blueberry
Barbecue Sauce 105

Chicken, Fig, and
Pancetta Rolls 107

Chicken Thighs with Cherry
Port Sauce 109

Cornish Game Hens Glazed with
Red Curry and Honey 111

Gingersnap and Mustard Chicken
with Bourbon Sauce 112

Turkey Breast with Blackberry
Ancho Sauce 113

Turkey, Sage, and Pomegranate
Meat Loaf 115

This chapter starts with recipes for two of my favorite ingredients: bacon and tasso. I use them over and over in my everyday cooking, and they are so easy to make at home.

A lot of the sauces in this chapter can be used interchangeably with other meats, and even with salmon. For example, I use the Pork Tenderloin with Raspberry Chipotle Sauce's (page 102) sweet, smoky sauce on salmon and chicken all the time. The same goes for the sauces from the Spare Ribs with Blueberry Barbecue Sauce (page 105) recipe and the Turkey Breast with Blackberry Ancho Sauce (page 113) recipe. Have fun experimenting with various sauce and protein combinations.

Many of these sauces and stuffings can be prepared two or three days in advance and refrigerated until you are ready to grill, making these dishes perfect for dinner parties. Just make sure that everything is at room temperature before being placed on the grill to ensure even grilling.

Homemade Bacon

Bacon is nothing more than pork belly that has been cured and then smoked. You won't believe how much better homemade bacon is—and it's so easy. Best of all, there are no preservatives or nitrates to worry about. Try plank-grilling the bacon on maple or apple wood planks if you can find them. Those woods add a sweet, smoky flavor that just takes this bacon over the top. And feel free to play around with the cure ingredients—substitute maple syrup, pomegranate syrup, brown sugar, or molasses for the honey; thyme, coriander, celery seed, juniper berries, chile peppers, coffee grounds, and citrus zest are alternative seasoning options.

• In a small bowl, combine the salt, bay leaves, onion powder, garlic powder, fennel, and pepper. Set aside.

• Place the pork belly in a large ziplock bag and pour half of the honey over one side of the pork, spreading with your hands or a spatula to make sure it is completely covered. Sprinkle half of the salt mixture over the honey. Flip the bag over and repeat with the remaining honey and salt mixture. Seal the bag tightly, squeezing out the excess air, and massage the pork belly between your hands until it is completely covered with the honey and salt mixture.

• Cure the pork in the refrigerator for 4 days until firm (it will get too salty if cured any longer). Flip the bag and massage the pork belly each day to make sure it is evenly coated with liquid and cure mixture. Do not drain the liquid.

continued

PLANK PREFERENCE: Maple

MAKES ABOUT 2 POUNDS

1 cup kosher salt
4 bay leaves, cut into slivers
1 tablespoon onion powder
1 tablespoon garlic powder
½ tablespoon ground fennel seeds
½ tablespoon freshly ground black pepper
2 pounds pork belly, any skin removed
1¼ cups honey

◆ Soak the plank for at least 12 hours and up to 24 hours. A well-soaked plank is highly recommended since this is a fatty cut of meat and flare-ups may occur.

◆ Remove the pork from the ziplock bag and rinse it under cool water, removing any cure from the surface of the pork. Pat the pork dry with paper towels.

◆ Prepare the plank for grilling according to the instructions on page 12. Place the pork on the toasted side of the plank. Close the lid and grill for 30 minutes, or until an instant-read thermometer inserted in the thickest part registers 150 degrees F.

◆ Remove the bacon from the plank and let it rest until it comes to room temperature, about 30 minutes, before slicing so that the juices do not leak out. At this point, the bacon can be sliced and fried. Alternatively, wrap the bacon well in plastic wrap and refrigerate for up to 2 weeks or freeze for up to 3 months.

Homemade Tasso

Tasso is Cajun ham that is found mostly in the cuisine of Louisiana. It tastes like a smoky, spicy, porky piece of goodness, and it's used mostly to flavor dishes like gumbo and jambalaya. I love it in so many other dishes as well, from scrambled eggs to creamy pastas. I even sprinkle it on salads, pizzas, and roasted vegetables. If a recipe calls for diced bacon or pancetta, try substituting tasso. Traditional tasso is cut into pieces about 4 to 5 inches long and 1 to 2 inches thick. Brining the pork before curing it with a spicy rub keeps it moist during plank grilling. It's a lengthy process, requiring two full days, but it's incredibly worth it!

• First, prepare the brine. In a large bowl, dissolve the salt and brown sugar in the boiling water. Add the cold water, garlic, peppercorns, dry mustard, and thyme sprigs and stir to combine. Add the pork slices, making sure they are submerged in the brine, cover, and refrigerate for 24 hours (they will get too salty if brined any longer). Remove the pork slices from the brine, rinse them well under cool water, and pat them dry with paper towels.

• Next, prepare the spice rub. In a large bowl, combine the paprika, chili powder, salt, onion powder, garlic powder, cinnamon, oregano, cayenne, red pepper flakes, and pepper. Add the pork slices and dredge well with the spice mixture until they are evenly coated. Place a cooling rack on a baking sheet and lay the pork slices on the rack. Refrigerate, uncovered, for another 24 hours.

continued

PLANK PREFERENCE: Oak

MAKES ABOUT 5 POUNDS

For the brine:
1 cup boiling water
¾ cup kosher salt
¾ cup packed brown sugar
4 cups cold water
4 cloves garlic, crushed
2 tablespoons black peppercorns
1 tablespoon dry mustard
1 bunch fresh thyme sprigs
5 pounds boneless pork butt, cut into 2-inch-thick slices

For the spice rub:
¼ cup paprika
2 tablespoons chili powder
1 tablespoon kosher salt
1 teaspoon onion powder
1 teaspoon garlic powder
1 teaspoon ground cinnamon
1 teaspoon dried oregano
½ teaspoon cayenne pepper (or to taste)
½ teaspoon crushed red pepper flakes
½ teaspoon freshly ground black pepper

◆ Soak the plank for at least 12 hours and up to 24 hours. A well-soaked plank is highly recommended since this is a fatty cut of meat and flare-ups may occur.

◆ Prepare the plank for grilling according to the instructions on page 12. Lay the pork slices on the toasted side of the plank. Close the lid and grill for 30 minutes, or until an instant-read thermometer inserted in the thickest part registers 160 degrees F.

◆ Remove the tasso from the plank and let it rest for 20 minutes. At this point, the tasso can be chopped and cooked. Alternatively, wrap the tasso well in plastic wrap and refrigerate for up to 2 weeks or freeze for up to 3 months.

Orange-Balsamic-Glazed Pork Chops Stuffed with Sweet Potatoes and Chorizo

Before I started plank grilling, I rarely grilled pork chops unless I brined them first—otherwise, they always seemed to dry out too quickly. Plank grilling eliminates that problem since the smoke helps the meat retain moisture. Sweet potatoes and cedar have a natural affinity for one another, the Spanish chorizo gives this dish a great kick, and the orange zest adds the perfect amount of freshness to bring out all the flavors. Be sure to zest the orange before juicing it.

- Soak the plank for at least 1 hour and up to 24 hours.

- First, prepare the stuffing. Line a large plate with a paper towel. Heat the oil in a large nonstick skillet over medium-high heat. Add the chorizo and sauté, stirring frequently, until browned, about 3 minutes. Using a slotted spoon, transfer the chorizo to the lined plate.

- Add the onion to the chorizo drippings in the pan and cook, scraping up any brown bits, until softened and translucent, about 5 minutes. Add the sweet potato, thyme, salt, and pepper. Reduce the heat to medium and cook, stirring occasionally, until the potatoes are tender, about 15 minutes. Add the chorizo and orange zest to the pan and stir to combine. Set aside to cool to room temperature.

continued

PLANK PREFERENCE:
Cedar, Alder, or Maple

MAKES 4 SERVINGS

For the stuffing:
1 teaspoon extra-virgin olive oil
3 ounces Spanish chorizo, cut into ¼-inch dice
1 small onion, finely chopped
1 small sweet potato (about ½ pound), peeled and cut into ¼-inch dice
1 teaspoon fresh thyme leaves, minced
½ teaspoon kosher salt
¼ teaspoon freshly ground black pepper
Zest of ½ orange (about 1 tablespoon)

For the glaze:
Juice of 1 orange (about ½ cup)
⅓ cup orange marmalade
¼ cup balsamic vinegar
¼ teaspoon kosher salt
¼ teaspoon freshly ground black pepper

4 (1¼-inch-thick) boneless pork
   loin chops
1 teaspoon kosher salt
½ teaspoon freshly ground black
   pepper

◆ Meanwhile, prepare the glaze. Combine the orange juice, marmalade, balsamic vinegar, salt, and pepper in a small heavy-bottomed saucepan. Bring to a boil over medium-high heat and cook until the glaze is slightly thickened and lightly coats the back of a spoon, 5 to 6 minutes.

◆ Season the pork chops with the salt and pepper. With a sharp boning knife, make a deep, centered cut into one side of each chop, creating a pocket. Divide the stuffing evenly among the chops, pressing the mixture firmly into the center pocket.

◆ Prepare the plank for grilling according to the instructions on page 12. Place the stuffed pork chops on the toasted side of the plank. Close the lid and grill for 20 to 25 minutes, or until an instant-read thermometer inserted in the thickest part registers 150 degrees F. Remove the pork chops from the grill and tent them with foil. Let them rest for 15 minutes. Drizzle with the glaze and serve.

Pork Chops Stuffed with Couscous, Peaches, and Bacon

PLANK PREFERENCE:
Cedar, Alder, or Maple

MAKES 4 SERVINGS

3 slices bacon, chopped

1 small onion, chopped

1 teaspoon rubbed dried sage

1½ teaspoons kosher salt

¾ teaspoon ground cinnamon

½ teaspoon freshly ground black pepper

⅓ cup low-sodium chicken stock

⅓ cup couscous

2 small peaches or 1 large peach, peeled, pitted, and cut into ¼-inch dice

4 (1¼-inch-thick) boneless pork loin chops

For the sauce:

½ cup Marsala wine

⅓ cup apricot preserves

1 tablespoon Dijon mustard

¼ teaspoon kosher salt

¼ teaspoon freshly ground black pepper

This stuffing is so delicious; I've used it to stuff chicken breasts as well. If you don't care for couscous, however, you can substitute rice, quinoa, bulgur, or any grain you prefer. Peaches can be difficult to peel—here's a helpful tip to make it easier: With a paring knife, cut an X at the bottom of the peach. Drop the peach in boiling water for 1 minute. Remove the peach from the hot water, submerge it immediately in ice-cold water for 1 minute, and then gently peel the skin away.

◆ Soak the plank for at least 1 hour and up to 24 hours.

◆ Heat a large skillet over medium heat. Add the bacon, onion, and sage and sauté, stirring occasionally, until the bacon is crispy and the onion has caramelized, about 15 minutes. Using a slotted spoon, transfer the bacon and onion mixture to a large bowl. Pour the fat from the skillet, but be sure to retain any tasty brown bits on the bottom of the skillet; they will be used later for the sauce. Set the skillet aside.

◆ In a small bowl, combine the salt, cinnamon, and pepper.

◆ In a small saucepan, bring the chicken stock and ½ teaspoon of the salt mixture to a boil over medium-high heat. Stir in the couscous, remove the pan from the heat, and cover. Let the saucepan sit undisturbed for 5 minutes, then remove the lid and fluff the couscous with a fork.

◆ Add the couscous, peaches, and ½ teaspoon of the salt mixture to the bacon and onion mixture. Set the stuffing aside to cool to room temperature.

• Meanwhile, prepare the sauce. Combine the wine, apricot preserves, mustard, salt, and pepper in the skillet used to cook the bacon and onions. Bring to a boil over medium-high heat, scraping up the brown bits from the pan for extra flavor. Cook until the sauce becomes thick and syrupy and lightly coats the back of a spoon, 2 to 3 minutes.

• Season the pork chops with the remaining 1¾ teaspoons salt mixture. With a sharp boning knife, make a deep, centered cut into one side of each chop, creating a pocket. Divide the stuffing evenly among the chops, pressing the mixture firmly into the center pocket.

• Prepare the plank for grilling according to the instructions on page 12. Place the stuffed pork chops on the toasted side of the plank. Close the lid and grill for 20 minutes, or until an instant-read thermometer inserted in the thickest part registers 150 degrees F. Remove the pork chops from the grill and tent them with foil. Let them rest for 10 minutes. Drizzle with the sauce and serve.

Pork Loin with Dried Plums and Soy Caramel Sauce

MAKES 4 TO 6 SERVINGS

½ teaspoon kosher salt

¼ teaspoon freshly ground black pepper

¼ teaspoon dried thyme

1 (2-pound) pork loin roast, trimmed of excess fat

10 pitted dried plums (about ½ cup)

For the sauce:

½ cup sugar

2 teaspoons freshly grated ginger

2 cloves garlic, minced

¼ cup low-sodium soy sauce

2 tablespoons unseasoned rice vinegar

½ cup water

¼ teaspoon Chinese five-spice powder

I love the contrasts of this dish: soft and gooey plums, crispy plank-grilled pork loin, and sweet and salty sauce. It is really important to make sure the dried plums (also known as prunes) are stuffed deep inside the pork loin so they don't pop out and become dry and chewy during grilling.

◆ Soak the plank for at least 1 hour and up to 24 hours.

◆ In a small bowl, combine the salt, pepper, and thyme. Rub the pork loin all over with the seasoning mixture. Using a small, sharp paring knife, make 10 deep slits randomly throughout the pork loin and stuff each slit with a dried plum, making sure none of the plums are sticking out. Let the pork loin sit at room temperature for 30 minutes before grilling.

◆ Meanwhile, prepare the sauce. In a deep, heavy-bottomed saucepan (about 8 inches wide and 4 inches deep), cook the sugar over medium heat, swirling the pan gently to make sure the sugar caramelizes evenly, until it turns auburn brown in color, 7 to 10 minutes. (If you stir the sugar, it can crystallize.) Remove the pan from the heat and stir in the ginger, garlic, soy sauce, vinegar, and water. Be careful—the mixture will bubble up violently. Increase the heat to medium-high and return the saucepan to the heat. Stir in the Chinese five-spice powder and bring to a boil. Cook, stirring occasionally, until the sauce thickens slightly and lightly coats the back of a spoon, about 2 minutes. Remove the pan from the heat and let the sauce cool to room temperature. The sauce can be prepared and refrigerated 1 day in advance.

◆ Prepare the plank for grilling according to the instructions on page 12. Place the pork on the toasted side of the plank. Close the lid and grill for 35 to 40 minutes, or until an instant-read thermometer inserted in the thickest part registers 155 degrees F. Remove the pork loin from the grill and tent it with foil. Let it rest for 15 minutes. Cut the pork crosswise into ⅓-inch-thick slices, arrange them on a platter, and drizzle with the sauce.

Pork Tenderloin with Raspberry Chipotle Sauce

PLANK PREFERENCE:
Cedar, Alder, or Maple

MAKES 4 TO 6 SERVINGS

For the sauce:

1 tablespoon extra-virgin olive oil

1 cup chopped onion

6 ounces raspberries (about 1½ cups)

½ cup sugar

¼ cup cider vinegar

1½ teaspoons chopped canned chipotle chiles in adobo

½ teaspoon kosher salt

½ teaspoon freshly ground black pepper

. . . .

1 teaspoon dried oregano

1 teaspoon kosher salt

½ teaspoon freshly ground black pepper

2 (1-pound) pork tenderloins, trimmed of excess fat

The smoky, spicy, chocolaty flavor of chipotle chiles, combined with the sweetness of raspberries, makes for an intensely flavored sauce that goes really well with pork tenderloin. This sauce also goes well with chicken, steak, salmon, hamburgers . . . you get the idea. It's that good. This recipe calls for only a small amount of canned chipotle chile in adobo; you can store the remainder in the refrigerator for up to 2 weeks, or you can freeze it for up to 6 months.

◆ Soak the plank for at least 1 hour and up to 24 hours.

◆ To prepare the sauce, heat the oil in a medium saucepan over medium-high heat. Add the onion and sauté until it is soft and translucent, about 3 minutes. Add the raspberries, sugar, vinegar, chipotles, salt, and pepper and bring to a boil. Reduce the heat to medium and simmer, stirring often, for 8 to 10 minutes, or until the mixture has thickened.

◆ Transfer the sauce to a blender and puree until smooth. Be careful while blending the hot sauce, as it needs room for steam to escape; remove or open the center part of the blender lid and cover it with a damp towel while blending. Using a spatula or the back of a spoon, push the sauce through a fine-mesh sieve into a small bowl, discarding the solids. Set aside.

◆ In a small bowl, combine the oregano, salt, and pepper. Rub the pork tenderloins all over with the seasoning mixture.

◆ Prepare the plank for grilling according to the instructions on page 12. Spread the sauce over all sides of the pork tenderloin with a pastry brush, reserving a small amount. Place the pork on the toasted side of the plank. Close the lid and grill for 15 to 20 minutes, or until an instant-read thermometer inserted in the thickest part registers 145 degrees F for medium or 160 degrees F for well-done. Brush the tenderloins all over with additional sauce and let them rest for 10 minutes before slicing.

. . . .

NOTE: Chipotle chiles are smoked and dried jalapeño chiles, and they are often packed in a spicy tomato sauce called adobo. You can find them in small cans in the Mexican food section of the grocery store or in Latin markets.

Spare Ribs with Blueberry Barbecue Sauce

I use two techniques to cook ribs for ultimate tenderness and flavor. First the ribs are baked low and slow in the oven, where much of the fat melts away and is discarded. Then they are crisped, smoked, and flavored on the plank before serving. The Blueberry Barbecue Sauce gives them a sweet and spicy kick and is a delicious twist on traditional barbecue sauce. The results are wonderfully sticky ribs.

• Soak the plank for at least 1 hour and up to 24 hours.

• In a small bowl, combine the chili powder, salt, and pepper. Rub the ribs all over with the seasoning mixture. Place on a large plate, cover with plastic wrap, and refrigerate for at least 4 hours and up to 24 hours.

• To make the sauce, heat the oil in a saucepan over medium-high heat. Add the onion, jalapeño, garlic powder, cumin, coriander, salt, and pepper and sauté until the vegetables soften, about 3 minutes. Stir in the blueberries, molasses, chili sauce, and vinegar and bring to a boil. Reduce the heat to medium and simmer, stirring occasionally, until the sauce thickens slightly, about 30 minutes.

• Transfer the sauce to a blender and puree until smooth. Be careful while blending the sauce, as it needs room for steam to escape; remove or open the center part of the blender lid and cover it with a damp towel while blending. The sauce can be prepared and refrigerated up to 3 days in advance.

continued

PLANK PREFERENCE:
Cedar, Alder, or Maple

MAKES 4 TO 6 SERVINGS

1 tablespoon chili powder
1 tablespoon kosher salt
1½ teaspoons freshly ground black pepper
1 slab pork spare ribs (3 to 4 pounds)

For the sauce:
1 tablespoon extra-virgin olive oil
½ cup diced onion
1 jalapeño, seeded and minced
½ teaspoon garlic powder
¼ teaspoon ground cumin
¼ teaspoon ground coriander
¼ teaspoon kosher salt
¼ teaspoon freshly ground black pepper
10 ounces fresh or frozen blueberries (about 2 cups)
½ cup molasses
¼ cup chili sauce
2 tablespoons cider vinegar

◆ When you are ready to cook the ribs, bring them to room temperature. Preheat the oven to 300 degrees F. Place the ribs in a baking pan, cover them with foil, and bake until tender, about 1½ hours. Once the ribs are cool enough to handle, remove them from the pan and generously brush each side of the ribs with ¼ cup of the sauce.

◆ Prepare the plank for grilling according to the instructions on page 12. Place the ribs on the toasted side of the plank. Close the lid and grill for 15 to 20 minutes, or until the ribs are crisp and lightly charred. Remove the ribs from the heat and brush with another ¼ cup of the sauce. Cut the ribs apart and serve immediately with additional sauce on the side.

Chicken, Fig, and Pancetta Rolls

I am a kebab fanatic. If there is a cooking class on kebabs, I will take it. If there is a cookbook on kebabs, I will buy it. I love the concept of skewering all types of flavors together to form one mouthwatering meal. This elegant dish showcases the contrasting flavors presented when the spicy smokiness of cedar, the sweetness of figs, the mellowness of chicken, the savory saltiness of pancetta, and the tartness of balsamic vinegar meld together beautifully. Dried apricots can be substituted for the figs if you prefer. To make these kebabs, you'll need four bamboo skewers, soaked in water for 1 hour. Or, if you prefer, you can use metal skewers.

◆ Soak plank for at least 1 hour and up to 24 hours.

◆ Bring the water to a boil in a small saucepan. Reduce the heat to low, add the figs, and cook for 8 to 10 minutes, or until they become plump. Drain the figs and set aside to cool.

◆ In a small saucepan, combine ½ cup of balsamic vinegar, wine, lemon juice, and maple syrup. Bring to a boil over medium heat and boil until the mixture is reduced by half and becomes syrupy, about 10 minutes. Cover the glaze to keep it warm.

continued

PLANK PREFERENCE: Cedar

MAKES 4 SERVINGS

2 cups water

10 dried figs, halved

½ cup plus 1 tablespoon balsamic vinegar, divided

½ cup white wine

Juice of ½ large lemon (about 2 tablespoons)

2 tablespoons maple syrup

1 tablespoon extra-virgin olive oil

1 teaspoon chopped fresh thyme

½ teaspoon kosher salt

¼ teaspoon freshly ground black pepper

2 boneless, skinless chicken breasts, cut into 1-inch cubes (about 20 pieces)

20 thin slices pancetta, or 10 bacon slices, cut in half

◆ In a large bowl, whisk the remaining 1 tablespoon of balsamic vinegar with the oil, thyme, salt, and pepper. Add the chicken and toss to coat.

◆ Next, prepare the skewers. Place a fig half on each piece of chicken, wrap it with 1 slice of the pancetta, and thread it securely on a skewer. Repeat until all the pieces are skewered (5 pieces per skewer), leaving ¼ inch between each chicken roll.

◆ Prepare the plank for grilling according to the instructions on page 12. Place the skewers on the toasted side of the plank. Close the lid and grill for 10 minutes, or until the chicken rolls are golden brown and cooked through.

◆ Allow the chicken rolls to sit for 10 minutes before removing them from the skewers. Arrange them on a serving platter and drizzle with the glaze. Alternatively, the glaze can be served as a dip on the side.

Chicken Thighs with Cherry Port Sauce

The deep, rich cherry and port flavors in this sauce are perfect with the dark meat of chicken thighs, but they also work well with duck, pork, beef, and salmon. Cherry season is short in California, usually only about six weeks, starting in mid-May through the end of June, so I often substitute frozen cherries to make this sauce year-round. Bing and Hudson cherries work best. The sauce can be prepared and refrigerated up to 3 days in advance.

◆ Soak the plank for at least 1 hour and up to 24 hours.

◆ Heat the oil in a saucepan over medium-high heat. Add the shallot, jalapeño, ½ teaspoon of the salt, and ¼ teaspoon of the pepper and cook, stirring often, until the vegetables are softened, about 3 minutes. Add the cherries, port, chicken stock, marmalade, balsamic vinegar, and sage and bring to a boil. Reduce the heat to medium and cook, stirring occasionally, for 30 minutes, or until the sauce has reduced and thickened slightly. Set aside.

◆ Season the chicken with the remaining ½ teaspoon of salt and ¼ teaspoon of pepper.

◆ Prepare the plank for grilling according to the instructions on page 12. Place the chicken on the toasted side of the plank. Close the lid and grill for 15 minutes. Spoon the sauce over the chicken, reserving a small amount for serving. Close the lid and grill for another 15 minutes, or until an instant-read thermometer inserted in the thickest part (but not touching the bone) registers 165 degrees F. Allow the chicken to rest for 10 minutes before serving with the remaining sauce.

PLANK PREFERENCE: Cedar, Alder, Maple, or Cherry

MAKES 4 SERVINGS

1 tablespoon extra-virgin olive oil
1 shallot, finely chopped
1 jalapeño, seeded and finely chopped
1 teaspoon kosher salt, divided
½ teaspoon freshly ground black pepper, divided
10 ounces fresh or frozen cherries, pitted and quartered (about 2 cups)
½ cup ruby port
½ cup low-sodium chicken stock
⅓ cup orange marmalade
2 tablespoons balsamic vinegar
1 tablespoon chopped fresh sage
8 bone-in, skinless chicken thighs (about 3 pounds)

Cornish Game Hens Glazed with Red Curry and Honey

My mom is an amazing cook who never believed in cooking from a can—everything had to be fresh from the market and made from scratch. I try to live my life that way as well, but sometimes, convenience is a bigger priority. While my mom would have made her own curry paste for this dish, it is so simple to use a good packaged curry paste (I use Thai Kitchen brand). Served with a side of basmati rice and a nice green salad, this is an easy dinner to prepare. Wrap any leftover ginger in plastic wrap and put it in the freezer. That way it doesn't go to waste, and you can just pull it out of the freezer and grate it anytime you need it.

- Soak the plank for at least 1 hour and up to 24 hours.

- Season the game hens with the salt and pepper. Let them sit at room temperature for 30 minutes.

- Meanwhile, in a medium bowl, whisk together the honey, soy sauce, red curry paste, garlic, and ginger. Set aside.

- Prepare the plank for grilling according to the instructions on page 12. Place the game hens, skin side up, on the toasted side of the plank. Close the lid and grill for 20 minutes. Brush the hens with half of the glaze, then close the lid and grill for another 25 to 30 minutes, or until an instant-read thermometer inserted in the inner thigh near the breast (but not touching the bone) registers 165 degrees F and the juices run clear. Transfer the game hens from the grill to a serving platter and brush with the remaining glaze. Let the hens rest for 10 minutes before serving.

PLANK PREFERENCE:
Cedar, Alder, or Maple

MAKES 4 SERVINGS

2 Cornish game hens, halved lengthwise
1½ teaspoons kosher salt
½ teaspoon freshly ground black pepper
¼ cup honey
¼ cup low-sodium soy sauce
1 tablespoon Thai red curry paste (or to taste, see note)
2 cloves garlic, minced
2 teaspoons freshly grated ginger

NOTE: Thai red curry paste comes in a variety of heat levels, so taste as you go, adding just 1 teaspoon at a time until the glaze reaches your desired spice level.

Gingersnap and Mustard Chicken with Bourbon Sauce

PLANK PREFERENCE:
Cedar, Alder, or Maple

MAKES 4 SERVINGS

For the sauce:

1 tablespoon extra-virgin olive oil

1 shallot, finely diced

1 cup low-sodium chicken stock

¼ cup bourbon

¼ cup low-sodium soy sauce

¼ cup packed light brown sugar

¼ teaspoon freshly ground black pepper

2 teaspoons cornstarch

2 teaspoons water

. . . .

4 (6- to 8-ounce) boneless, skinless chicken breasts

1 teaspoon kosher salt

½ teaspoon freshly ground black pepper

¼ cup Dijon mustard

1½ cups crushed gingersnaps (from about 3 cups gingersnap cookies—I prefer Nabisco brand)

My friend Becky Elkins is a great baker, and every once in a while we get together and bake. One day she was telling me that she had made chicken with a gingersnap and mustard crust for her family the night before, and while it had nothing to do with baking, it piqued my interest. I tried my own plank-grilled version right away, and this simple dish turned out so well that it's become a regular feature on my home menu. By the way, this crust also tastes great on pork chops.

◆ Soak the plank for at least 1 hour and up to 24 hours.

◆ To make the sauce, in a small saucepan, heat the oil over medium-high heat. Add the shallot and cook, stirring occasionally, until softened and translucent, about 3 minutes. Add the chicken stock, bourbon, soy sauce, brown sugar, and pepper and bring to a boil. Reduce the heat to medium and cook until the sauce has reduced to 1 cup, 10 to 12 minutes. In a small bowl, combine the cornstarch and water. Stir the slurry into the bourbon sauce and cook until thickened, about 1 minute. Remove the pan from the heat.

◆ Meanwhile, season the chicken with the salt and pepper. Using a pastry brush, cover the chicken with the mustard, then dredge in the gingersnap crumbs. Set aside.

◆ Prepare the plank for grilling according to the instructions on page 12. Place the chicken on the toasted side of the plank. Close the lid and grill for 15 to 20 minutes, or until an instant-read thermometer inserted in the thickest part registers 165 degrees F. Let the chicken rest for 10 minutes before slicing. Drizzled with the sauce and serve.

Turkey Breast with Blackberry Ancho Sauce

Plank-grilled turkey is one of the most delicious things you will ever eat. If I could fit an entire turkey on a plank, I would. But the turkey breast is my favorite part, and this dish satisfies my cravings. The sauce can be made up to 2 days ahead of time and stored in the refrigerator. It's delicious on beef, pork, chicken, or salmon.

PLANK PREFERENCE:
Cedar, Alder, or Maple

MAKES 6 TO 8 SERVINGS

♦ Soak the plank for at least 1 hour and up to 24 hours.

♦ In a small bowl, stir together the oil, garlic, salt, pepper, oregano, and dry mustard. Brush the mixture over the turkey and rub it under the skin. Let the turkey sit at room temperature for 30 minutes, or refrigerate for up to 24 hours, removing it from the refrigerator 30 minutes before grilling.

♦ Meanwhile, prepare the sauce. Drain the chiles, reserving the soaking water, and stem, seed, and roughly chop them. Place the chiles in a blender with the reserved water and puree until smooth. Strain the ancho puree through a fine-mesh sieve into a medium bowl and set aside.

continued

2 tablespoons extra-virgin olive oil
2 cloves garlic, minced
2 teaspoons kosher salt
1 teaspoon freshly ground black pepper
1 teaspoon dried oregano
½ teaspoon dry mustard
1 bone-in, skin-on turkey breast half (about 3½ pounds)

For the sauce:
2 large dried ancho chiles, soaked in 1 cup boiling water for 30 minutes
2 tablespoons extra-virgin olive oil
1 small onion, finely chopped
2 cloves garlic, minced
1 tablespoon unsweetened cocoa powder
½ teaspoon kosher salt
¼ teaspoon freshly ground black pepper
¼ teaspoon cayenne pepper
½ cup sugar
12 ounces fresh blackberries (about 2 cups)
Juice of 2 large limes (about 4 tablespoons)

◆ Heat the oil in a medium saucepan over medium heat. Add the onion and sauté until softened and translucent, 5 to 7 minutes. Add the garlic, cocoa powder, salt, pepper, and cayenne and cook, stirring, for 1 minute. Add the ancho puree, sugar, blackberries, and lime juice and bring to a boil over medium-high heat. Reduce the heat to medium and simmer, mashing the berries occasionally with the back of a spoon, for 20 minutes, or until the berries break down.

◆ Transfer the sauce to the blender in 2 batches so that the steam does not cause the lid to pop off and puree until smooth. Strain through a fine-mesh sieve back into the medium bowl that held the ancho puree and set aside.

◆ Prepare the plank for grilling according to the instructions on page 12. Place the turkey on the toasted side of the plank. Close the lid and grill for 20 minutes. Brush ⅓ cup of the sauce over the turkey, close the lid, and grill for another 20 minutes, or until an instant-read thermometer inserted in the thickest part registers 165 degrees F. Remove the turkey from the grill and let it rest for 15 minutes before slicing. Serve with the remaining sauce.

Turkey, Sage, and Pomegranate Meat Loaf

Meat loaf gets transformed when it's plank-grilled, as it soaks up the smoke and wood flavors and the edges get really crunchy and caramelized from the grilling. Ever since discovering this little known fact, I've been experimenting with different meat loaves, and the lightness of this version makes it my favorite. I also substitute raw oats for the traditional bread or bread crumb filler, making it naturally gluten-free. When pomegranates are in season, be sure to include the pomegranate seeds; when they're not, dried cranberries are a great substitute.

1 tablespoon extra-virgin olive oil

1 large onion, chopped

2 cloves garlic, minced

2 teaspoons freshly grated ginger

1 teaspoon kosher salt

½ teaspoon freshly ground black pepper

1 teaspoon rubbed dried sage, divided

⅓ cup low-sodium chicken stock

1 tablespoon tomato paste

1¼ pounds ground turkey

1 pound sweet Italian turkey sausage, casings removed

1 cup pomegranate seeds (about ½ large pomegranate)

¾ cup old-fashioned oats

2 large eggs, beaten

1 tablespoon Worcestershire sauce

½ cup ketchup

♦ Soak the plank for at least 1 hour and up to 24 hours.

♦ In a large sauté pan, heat the oil over medium-high heat. Add the onion and cook, stirring occasionally, until softened and translucent, 5 to 6 minutes. Add the garlic, ginger, salt, pepper, and ½ teaspoon of the sage and cook for 1 minute. Add the chicken stock and tomato paste and mix well. Set aside to cool to room temperature.

♦ In a large bowl, combine the turkey, turkey sausage, pomegranate seeds, oats, eggs, Worcestershire sauce, and the onion mixture. Mix gently until combined, being careful not to overwork the meat (if you do, the meat loaf will be tough). To test for seasoning, cook 1 teaspoon of the meat loaf mixture in a hot skillet. Adjust the seasoning if needed.

continued

◆ In a small bowl, mix the ketchup and the remaining ½ teaspoon of sage. Set aside.

◆ Prepare the plank for grilling according to the instructions on page 12. Spoon the meat loaf mixture onto the toasted side of the plank and form it into a 9-by-4-inch loaf. Carefully spoon the ketchup mixture over the meat loaf. Close the lid and grill for 20 to 25 minutes, or until an instant-read thermometer inserted in the thickest part registers 160 degrees F. Remove the plank from the grill and let the meat loaf rest for 10 minutes before serving.

BEEF & LAMB

Tri-Tip Rubbed with
Chocolate and Espresso 119

Flank Steak Stuffed with
Artichokes and Brie 121

Chicken-Planked Steak 123

Meat Loaf with Tomato and Red
Pepper Sauce 125

Stuffed Meatball Sliders 127

Mongolian Veal Chops 130

Laura's Chili 132

Lamb Shoulder Chops with
Tamarind Apricot Glaze 134

Rack of Lamb with Rosemary
Pomegranate Sauce 137

Lamb and Dried Cherry
Meatballs 138

This chapter, more than any other, relies on planks other than cedar. Cedar still works—it always does—to create a wonderful plank-grilled meal. But if you can find oak, mesquite, or hickory woods for the beef dishes, or cherrywood for the lamb dishes, you will experience these meals in a whole new way. The robust, smoky quality of oak, mesquite, or hickory paired with beef is a combination made for the ages. Laura's Chili (page 132) takes one of my favorite go-to dinners and turns it into something you will remember long after your meal is over.

Another of my favorite recipes in this chapter is the Chicken-Planked Steak (page 123). It epitomizes taking a classic dish that we all grew up with and giving it a twist that takes it from satisfying to extraordinary. And like so many other plank-grilled dishes, it tastes great not because of added fat, but because it soaks up all those amazing flavors of wood and smoke.

Plank grilling isn't just for American food. More and more of us are experimenting with spices and loving what we're discovering. The Lamb Shoulder Chops with Tamarind Apricot Glaze (page 134) recipe uses tamarind concentrate and the Indian spice garam masala. Combining those wonderful Indian seasonings with the aroma and flavors of wood and smoke makes for an unforgettable meal.

Tri-Tip Rubbed with Chocolate and Espresso

Chocolate, coffee, and beef are a match made in heaven. This rub is so simple, yet it adds an incredible depth of flavor to this tri-tip when paired with the flavors of smoke and wood. Tri-tip is triangular in shape, comes from the bottom sirloin, and is very popular in California. It is also called sirloin tip, triangle steak, Santa Maria–style roast, or culotte steak. If tri-tip isn't available in your area, you can substitute a top sirloin roast. If you have Starbucks VIA Ready Brew Coffee in your pantry, it can be substituted for the instant espresso powder.

◆ Soak the plank for at least 1 hour and up to 24 hours.

◆ In a small bowl, mix together the brown sugar, espresso powder, chili powder, salt, pepper, cocoa powder, onion powder, garlic powder, and cayenne. Rub the spice mixture all over the tri-tip. Refrigerate for at least 4 hours and up to 24 hours. Remove the tri-tip from the refrigerator and let it sit at room temperature for 45 minutes before grilling.

◆ Prepare the plank for grilling according to the instructions on page 12. Place the tri-tip on the toasted side of the plank. Close the lid and grill for 40 minutes, or until an instant-read thermometer inserted into the thickest part registers 130 degrees F for medium-rare or 145 degrees F for medium. Transfer the tri-tip to a cutting board and tent it with foil. Let the meat rest for 15 to 30 minutes before slicing.

PLANK PREFERENCE: Oak

MAKES 8 SERVINGS

2 tablespoons packed brown sugar

1 tablespoon instant espresso powder

1 tablespoon chili powder

1 tablespoon kosher salt

1½ teaspoons freshly ground black pepper

1 teaspoon unsweetened cocoa powder

1 teaspoon onion powder

1 teaspoon garlic powder

½ teaspoon cayenne pepper

1 (4½-pound) tri-tip, trimmed of excess fat

Flank Steak Stuffed with Artichokes and Brie

I like to make this dish for dinner parties; stuffed roasts always make a great presentation. It feeds a lot of people and, served over mashed potatoes or rice, makes a delicious meal. Even better, the stuffing can be made a day in advance and kept in the refrigerator, making preparation that much easier. You do not want to overcook flank steak because it can get tough, so be sure to have a meat thermometer on hand. Also be aware that you will need butcher's twine for this recipe.

◆ Soak the plank for at least 1 hour and up to 24 hours.

◆ In a small bowl, combine the herbes de Provence, salt, and pepper.

◆ Place the artichoke hearts, Brie, sun-dried tomatoes, garlic, shallot, basil, oil, vinegar, and 1½ teaspoons of the seasoning mixture in the bowl of a food processor and pulse 8 to 10 times, until combined but still a little chunky.

◆ Season both sides of the steak with the remaining 1¾ teaspoons of the seasoning mixture. Lay the steak on a flat work surface and spread the stuffing evenly over the steak, leaving a 1-inch border all the way around. Starting at the long end closest to you, roll the steak firmly, jelly roll style—up and away from you, being careful not to squeeze the filling out of the sides. Once the steak is rolled, tie it with butcher's twine, securing at 1-inch increments to hold the steak together.

continued

MAKES 6 TO 8 SERVINGS

1 teaspoon herbes de Provence

1½ teaspoons kosher salt

¾ teaspoon freshly ground black pepper

1 (14-ounce) can quartered artichoke hearts, drained and coarsely chopped

8 ounces Brie, rind removed, cut into ½-inch cubes

½ cup julienned dehydrated sun-dried tomatoes

2 cloves garlic, finely chopped

1 shallot, finely chopped

¼ cup chopped fresh basil

2 tablespoons extra-virgin olive oil

2 tablespoons red wine vinegar

1 (2½-pound) flank steak, trimmed of excess fat, butterflied, and pounded thin (1¼ inch thick) (see note, page 122)

◆ Prepare the plank for grilling according to the instructions on page 12. Carefully place the stuffed flank steak, seam side down, on the toasted side of the plank. Close the lid and grill for 40 to 45 minutes, or until an instant-read thermometer inserted in the thickest part registers 140 degrees F. Let the meat rest for 15 minutes before slicing. When it is time to serve, remove the butcher's twine and cut the steak into 1-inch-thick slices.

. . . .

NOTE: Many butchers will butterfly your steak for you, but it's quite easy to do it yourself. Cut the steak in half horizontally, keeping one long side attached. Open the halves like a book so that the flank steak is one long rectangular piece, and pound lightly with a meat pounder or rolling pin until the steak is an even thickness all over.

Chicken-Planked Steak

Sometimes all I want is simple comfort food. Chicken-fried steak is one of my favorites, but as with most comfort foods, it's not exactly healthy. One of the great things about plank grilling is that it eliminates the fat used when frying these steaks. Instead, you get the incredible flavor of aromatic smoke and wood, with no additional calories. Cornflakes are the other secret—their subtle sweetness is the perfect counterbalance to the smoke and helps add to the crunchiness of this dish.

- ◆ Soak the plank for at least 1 hour and up to 24 hours.

- ◆ In a small bowl, combine the salt, garlic powder, onion powder, pepper, and cayenne.

- ◆ Set up an assembly line of 3 pie plates. In the first pie plate, combine the flour with 1 teaspoon of the seasoning mixture. In the second pie plate, whisk the eggs, milk, and 1 teaspoon of the seasoning mixture. In the third pie plate, combine the cornflakes with 1 teaspoon of the seasoning mixture.

- ◆ Reserve 1 teaspoon of the seasoning mixture for later use in the sauce. Season the cube steaks with the remaining 1¼ teaspoons seasoning mixture. Dredge a steak in the flour mixture, patting off any excess, then dip it in the egg mixture. Finally, dredge it in the cornflake mixture, pressing lightly to coat, then transfer the steak to a large plate. Repeat with the remaining steaks.

continued

PLANK PREFERENCE: Oak

MAKES 4 SERVINGS

2 teaspoons kosher salt
1 teaspoon garlic powder
1 teaspoon onion powder
1 teaspoon freshly ground black pepper
¼ teaspoon cayenne pepper
½ cup all-purpose flour
2 large eggs
¼ cup skim milk
3 cups cornflakes, crushed
4 (4-ounce) cube steaks
Olive oil cooking spray

For the sauce:
1 teaspoon extra-virgin olive oil
3 ounces Spanish chorizo, finely diced
1 tablespoon Dijon mustard
2 tablespoons all-purpose flour
1½ cups skim milk

• Prepare the plank for grilling according to the instructions on page 12. Place the steaks on the toasted side of the plank and spray them lightly with the cooking spray. Close the lid and grill for 15 to 20 minutes, or until golden brown and cooked through. Transfer the steaks from the plank to the grill grate right above the high flames and with the lid open, grill for 30 seconds, or until the bottom is crispy as well. Transfer the steaks to a platter and let them rest for 10 minutes.

• Meanwhile, prepare the sauce. Heat the oil in a heavy-bottomed saucepan over medium-high heat. Add the chorizo and cook, stirring often, until browned, about 2 minutes. Reduce the heat to medium, add the mustard and the reserved 1 teaspoon of seasoning mixture, and stir to combine. Add the flour and cook for 1 minute, stirring often. Slowly whisk in the milk and cook until the mixture is thickened, about 2 minutes. Drizzle the sauce over the steaks and serve.

Meat Loaf with Tomato and Red Pepper Sauce

I never understood the big deal about meat loaf. It is my husband's favorite meal on earth, and I would reluctantly make it once a year on his birthday. Then I tried plank-grilling meat loaf and now I am hooked. I love this recipe—the smoke and wood flavors permeate the meat loaf, bacon, and sauce as they grill. This recipe takes a while to prepare since there are a lot of vegetables that need chopping and sautéing, but the time required is very much worthwhile. You can make the sauce up to 3 days in advance.

* Soak the plank for at least 1 hour and up to 24 hours.

* To make the sauce, in a medium saucepan over medium-high heat, combine the ketchup, tomatoes, bell pepper, onion, garlic, vinegar, Worchestershire sauce, parsley, dry mustard, salt, and pepper and bring to a boil. Reduce the heat to medium and simmer for 7 minutes, or until the sauce is slightly thickened. Set aside.

* Next, prepare the meat loaf. Heat the oil in a large non-stick skillet over medium heat. Add the onion, bell pepper, and celery and cook, stirring occasionally, until the vegetables are softened and beginning to brown around the edges, about 5 minutes. Add the garlic, mushrooms, thyme, and rosemary. Cook until any liquid has evaporated and the mushrooms are tender, 10 to 15 minutes. Remove the skillet from the heat and allow the vegetables to cool completely.

continued

PLANK PREFERENCE: Oak

MAKES 8 SERVINGS

For the sauce:
½ cup ketchup
2 plum tomatoes, diced
½ red bell pepper, chopped
½ cup chopped onion
2 large cloves garlic, minced
2 tablespoons red wine vinegar
2 tablespoons Worcestershire sauce
1 teaspoon chopped fresh flat-leaf parsley
1 teaspoon dry mustard
½ teaspoon kosher salt
¼ teaspoon freshly ground black pepper

. . . .

2 tablespoons extra-virgin olive oil
1½ cups finely chopped onion
½ red bell pepper, finely chopped
1 stalk celery, finely chopped
6 cloves garlic, minced
½ cup cremini mushrooms, finely chopped
1 teaspoon chopped fresh thyme, or ¼ teaspoon dried

1 teaspoon chopped fresh rosemary, or ¼ teaspoon dried

2 large eggs

½ cup milk

⅓ cup ketchup

2 teaspoons Dijon mustard

1 tablespoon Worcestershire
  sauce

1 teaspoon kosher salt

¼ teaspoon freshly ground black
  pepper

1 pound ground beef

½ pound ground veal

½ pound bulk Italian pork
  sausage

1 cup fresh bread crumbs (from
  about 2 to 3 slices, see note)

5 slices bacon, halved

. . . .

NOTE: The easiest way to prepare fresh bread crumbs is by taking a few slices of day-old French
or Italian bread, tearing them into
chunks, and pulsing them in a food
processor. There is no need to
remove the crusts.

◆ In a large bowl, whisk together the eggs, milk, ketchup,
mustard, Worcestershire sauce, salt, and pepper. Stir in
the vegetable mixture. Stir in the beef, veal, sausage,
and bread crumbs and mix until just combined. Do not
overmix or the meat will get tough. To test for seasoning,
cook 1 teaspoon of the meat loaf mixture in a hot skillet.
Adjust the seasoning if needed.

◆ Prepare the plank for grilling according to the instructions on page 12. Spoon the meat loaf mixture onto the
toasted side of the plank and form into a loaf. Arrange the
slices of bacon on top, then carefully spoon the sauce over
the meat loaf. Close the lid and grill for 1 hour and 10
minutes, or until an instant-read thermometer inserted
in the thickest part registers 160 degrees F. Remove the
plank from the grill and let the meat loaf rest for 10 minutes before serving.

Stuffed Meatball Sliders

This dish is a favorite with my son Andrew. He has no fear of meat juices and red sauce rolling down his chin and arms, landing on his freshly laundered shirt. I should stop making these so often to cut down on laundry, but they are just so scrumptious. Meatballs, like meat loaf, really soak up the flavors from the wood and smoke. I also love making these meatballs with turkey and turkey sausage, so if you're not a red meat eater, just substitute 1 pound of turkey for the beef and veal and ½ pound of turkey sausage for the pork sausage.

◆ Soak the plank for at least 1 hour and up to 24 hours.

◆ First, prepare the meatballs. In a large bowl, combine the beef, veal, sausage, bread crumbs, milk, egg, parsley, basil, salt, black pepper, and red pepper flakes and mix gently with a fork. With wet hands, lightly form the mixture into 8 balls. With your thumb, make an indentation in each meatball, insert a cheese cube into the center, and seal. Refrigerate the meatballs for 1 hour before grilling.

◆ Meanwhile, prepare the sauce. Heat the oil in a large, deep skillet over medium-high heat. Add the onion and sauté until softened, about 5 minutes. Add the tomatoes, sugar, salt, basil, pepper, and red pepper flakes and stir well. Bring the sauce to a simmer, reduce the heat to low, cover, and cook for 10 minutes. Keep the sauce covered while you grill the meatballs.

continued

MAKES 4 SERVINGS

For the meatballs:
½ pound ground beef
½ pound ground veal
½ pound bulk Italian pork
  sausage
½ cup fresh bread crumbs (see
  note, page 126)
¼ cup milk
1 large egg, lightly beaten
2 tablespoons chopped fresh
  flat-leaf parsley
1 teaspoon dried basil
1 teaspoon kosher salt
½ teaspoon freshly ground black
  pepper
¼ teaspoon crushed red pepper
  flakes
2 ounces mozzarella, cut into 8
  (½-inch) cubes

For the sauce:
2 tablespoons extra-virgin olive oil
1 small onion, finely chopped
1 (28-ounce) can crushed
  tomatoes
1 tablespoon sugar
1 teaspoon kosher salt
½ teaspoon dried basil
¼ teaspoon freshly ground black
  pepper
¼ teaspoon crushed red pepper
  flakes

• Prepare the plank for grilling according to the instructions on page 12. Place the meatballs on the toasted side of the plank. Close the lid and grill for 15 minutes, or until the meatballs are browned. Transfer the meatballs to the skillet with the sauce.

• To assemble the sliders, spoon a meatball and sauce onto each slider bun. Sprinkle with the parsley and serve immediately.

8 slider buns, buttered and toasted on the grill
2 tablespoons chopped fresh flat-leaf parsley or basil

Mongolian Veal Chops

PLANK PREFERENCE:
Cedar, Alder, or Maple

MAKES 4 SERVINGS

½ cup hoisin sauce
¼ cup plum sauce
1 tablespoon unseasoned rice vinegar
1 tablespoon low-sodium soy sauce
1 tablespoon sesame oil
2 cloves garlic, minced
2 teaspoons freshly grated ginger
1 teaspoon onion powder
½ teaspoon chili paste (I use *sambal oelek*)
4 (8-ounce) bone-in veal loin chops, about 1 inch thick
1 tablespoon toasted sesame seeds
1 tablespoon chopped green onions

The marinade for the veal goes great with pork chops and chicken breasts as well. I love the incredible flavor these chops get from the smoke and wood, but to get that crispy texture that I love in grilled chops, I take them off the plank at the end of the cooking time and grill them briefly on the grate over high flames. Delicious!

* Soak the plank for at least 1 hour and up to 24 hours.

* In a large bowl, combine the hoisin sauce, plum sauce, vinegar, soy sauce, sesame oil, garlic, ginger, onion powder, and chili paste. Add the veal chops and turn them to coat with the marinade. Cover and refrigerate for at least 4 hours and up to 24 hours. Let the veal chops sit at room temperature for 30 minutes before grilling.

* Prepare the plank for grilling according to the instructions on page 12. Remove the veal chops from the marinade and place them on the toasted side of the plank. Close the lid and grill for 15 to 20 minutes, or until an instant-read thermometer inserted in the thickest part registers 135 degrees F for medium-rare or 140 degrees F for medium. Transfer the veal chops from the plank to the grill grate right above the high flames and, with the lid open, grill for 30 seconds on each side, or until crispy. Transfer the veal chops to a platter and let them rest for 10 minutes before serving. Garnish with the sesame seeds and green onions.

Laura's Chili

MAKES 6 TO 8 SERVINGS

2½ pounds chuck roast

1 teaspoon kosher salt

½ teaspoon freshly ground black pepper

3 poblano chiles

6 plum tomatoes, halved

2 tablespoons chili powder

2 tablespoons unsweetened cocoa powder

1 tablespoon ground cumin

1 tablespoon sugar

2 teaspoons dried oregano

1 teaspoon dried thyme

½ teaspoon ground coriander

½ teaspoon ground cinnamon

⅛ teaspoon crushed red pepper flakes

3 tablespoons plus 1 teaspoon extra-virgin olive oil, divided

1 (14.5-ounce) can red kidney beans, rinsed and drained

1 (14.5-ounce) can white kidney beans, rinsed and drained

1 (14.5-ounce) can pinto beans, rinsed and drained

1 (14.5-ounce) can black beans, rinsed and drained

Most of us have a specialty that we like to cook; for my friend Laura Howell, it's chili. When I told her I would like to include a chili recipe in this book, she and I set out to come up with one that would most benefit from the flavors of wood and smoke. I may be biased, but I think that this is the best chili ever. It's best to use oak, hickory, or mesquite wood planks for this recipe since their strong, robust flavors work so well with beef.

◆ Soak the plank for at least 1 hour and up to 24 hours.

◆ Season the roast with the salt and pepper. Let it sit at room temperature for 45 minutes.

◆ Prepare the plank for grilling according to the instructions on page 12. Place the beef on the toasted side of the plank. Close the lid and grill for 30 minutes. The roast won't be tender at this point; you just want it to soak up the flavors from the wood and smoke. Transfer the beef to a cutting board to rest.

◆ Place the poblanos and tomatoes, cut side down, on the plank. You may need to overlap the vegetables a little to fit them all on the plank. Close the lid and grill for 20 minutes, or until the vegetables are tender. Transfer the poblanos to a large bowl and cover the bowl with plastic wrap. Place the tomatoes next to the beef on the cutting board. Let the vegetables cool for 10 minutes.

◆ Peel the skin off of the poblanos, cut them open, and remove some of the seeds (the more seeds you remove, the less spicy the chili will be). Roughly chop the poblanos and tomatoes and place them back in the large bowl, along with their juices. Chop the beef into ¼-inch dice and add it to the bowl.

• In a small bowl, combine the chili powder, cocoa powder, cumin, sugar, oregano, thyme, coriander, cinnamon, and red pepper flakes. Add 3 tablespoons of the oil and stir to combine. Set aside.

• Heat the remaining 1 teaspoon of oil in a large, heavy saucepan or Dutch oven over medium-high heat. Add the beef mixture and cook for 1 minute, stirring frequently. Add the red and white kidney beans, pinto beans, black beans, diced tomatoes, beef broth, and the spice mixture. Stir to combine and bring the chili to a simmer. Reduce the heat to low, cover, and cook, stirring occasionally, for 1 hour, or until the beef is tender. Serve garnished with the sour cream, grated cheddar, and red onion.

1 (28-ounce) can diced tomatoes
1 (10.5-ounce) can beef broth
Sour cream, for garnish
Grated cheddar, for garnish
Chopped red onion, for garnish

Lamb Shoulder Chops with Tamarind Apricot Glaze

PLANK PREFERENCE: Cherry

MAKES 4 SERVINGS

2 teaspoons garam masala
1 teaspoon kosher salt
4 (¼- to ½-inch-thick) lamb
  shoulder chops

For the glaze:
⅔ cup low-sodium chicken stock
¼ cup chopped dried apricots
1½ tablespoons tamarind
  concentrate
1 tablespoon molasses
2 cloves garlic, minced
¼ teaspoon kosher salt

This recipe uses a few ingredients that you may have to search for, but it is well worth the trouble. Garam masala is an Indian spice blend generally made up of black pepper, cardamom, cumin, cloves, and cinnamon. Tamarind concentrate is made from the tamarind pod, a plant used in many Thai and Indian recipes. It has a sour, fruity flavor that is difficult to duplicate. Be sure to use tamarind concentrate and not tamarind pulp. Tamarind pulp comes in a block and requires soaking in hot water, then straining to remove the seeds and skin. Tamarind concentrate cuts down on all that time since you don't have to soak and strain it. Both garam masala and tamarind concentrate can be found at Whole Foods and other specialty stores as well as at Indian markets. The sweet and sour flavors you get from the glaze, mixed with the aromatic smoke and wood, really bring out the best in the lamb.

◆ Soak the plank for at least 1 hour and up to 24 hours.

◆ In a small bowl, combine the garam masala and salt. Season the lamb chops with the mixture. Set aside.

◆ Next, prepare the glaze. Combine the chicken stock, apricots, tamarind concentrate, molasses, garlic, and salt in a medium saucepan. Bring to a boil over medium-high heat, then reduce the heat to medium and simmer for 10 minutes, or until the glaze is thickened and reduced by half. Transfer the glaze to the bowl of a food processor and blend until smooth. It will have the texture of a jam or paste. Let the glaze cool to room temperature, then brush it on both sides of the lamb chops.

◆ Prepare the plank for grilling according to the instructions on page 12. Place the lamb chops on the toasted side of the plank. Close the lid and grill for 15 minutes, or until an instant-read thermometer inserted in the thickest part registers 135 degrees F for medium-rare or 145 degrees F for medium. Remove the lamb chops from the grill and let them rest for 5 to 10 minutes before serving.

. . . .

NOTE: Shoulder chops are economical and have a robust lamb flavor, but they can be a little tough and chewy. For a more tender—albeit more pricey—chop, you can substitute lamb rib chops, which come from the center rib section of the lamb and have a long rib bone with the loin meat attached to the end. You can also substitute lamb loin chops, also more tender and pricey, but cut from between the ribs and back and look like little T-bone steaks. Both the rib chops and loin chops have substantially less meat on them than shoulder chops, so double the amount of total chops if you do choose to substitute.

Rack of Lamb with Rosemary Pomegranate Sauce

Pomegranate juice is readily available in local supermarkets. You can, however, substitute any unsweetened dark juice, such as cranberry, cran-apple, or even a good ruby port wine. If you do use pomegranate juice, this dish looks very festive garnished with pomegranate seeds when they are in season.

PLANK PREFERENCE: Cherry

MAKES 4 SERVINGS

1½ cups pomegranate juice, divided
¾ cup dry red wine, divided
2 tablespoons extra-virgin olive oil
Leaves from 1 sprig fresh rosemary
8-rib rack of lamb (1¼ to 1½ pounds), trimmed

For the sauce:
2 tablespoons unsalted butter
1 shallot, minced
1 cup beef broth
Juice of 1 large lemon (about 4 tablespoons)
2 tablespoons seedless raspberry jam
1 teaspoon Dijon mustard
1 teaspoon chopped fresh rosemary
1 teaspoon chopped fresh thyme
½ teaspoon kosher salt
¼ teaspoon freshly ground black pepper

Rosemary sprigs, for garnish

• Soak the plank for at least 1 hour and up to 24 hours.

• Combine ½ cup of the pomegranate juice and ¼ cup of the wine with the oil and rosemary in a large glass baking dish. Add the lamb and turn it to coat both sides with the marinade. Cover and refrigerate for at least 4 hours, turning the lamb occasionally. Let the lamb sit at room temperature for 30 minutes before grilling.

• To make the sauce, in a large skillet, melt the butter over medium heat. Add the shallot and sauté until translucent, about 2 minutes. Add the remaining 1 cup of pomegranate juice and ½ cup of wine, and the beef broth, lemon juice, jam, mustard, rosemary, and thyme and cook until the sauce is reduced by half and almost syrupy, about 20 minutes. Season with the salt and pepper. Set aside.

• Prepare the plank for grilling according to the instructions on page 12. Place the lamb on the toasted side of the plank. Close the lid and grill for 20 minutes, or until an instant-read thermometer inserted in the thickest part registers 135 degrees F for medium-rare. Transfer the lamb to a cutting board, tent it with foil, and allow it to rest for 5 minutes. Cut the lamb into double chops. To serve, spoon the sauce onto individual serving plates, place the lamb chops on top, and garnish with the rosemary sprigs.

Lamb and Dried Cherry Meatballs

PLANK PREFERENCE: Cherry

MAKES 4 SERVINGS

1 tablespoon extra-virgin olive oil

1 cup chopped onion

2 cloves garlic, minced

1 pound ground lamb

⅓ cup fresh bread crumbs (see
    note, page 126)

¼ cup dried cherries, finely
    chopped

2 tablespoons milk

2 tablespoons chopped fresh mint

1 large egg, lightly beaten

1 teaspoon kosher salt

½ teaspoon ground coriander

½ teaspoon ground fennel seeds

½ teaspoon freshly ground black
    pepper

These lamb meatballs are lush, fatty, juicy, and complexly flavored with fruity dried cherries, aromatic spices, and zesty mint. I like to serve these meatballs over a bed of couscous or in pita bread—vehicles that soak up the juices and showcase the meatballs at their best.

◆ Soak the plank for at least 1 hour and up to 24 hours.

◆ In a large nonstick skillet, heat the oil over medium-high heat. Add the onion and sauté, stirring occasionally, until softened and translucent, about 3 minutes. Add the garlic and cook for another 30 seconds. Remove the pan from the heat and let the vegetables cool to room temperature.

◆ In a large bowl, combine the lamb, bread crumbs, cherries, milk, mint, egg, salt, coriander, fennel seeds, pepper, and onion mixture and stir gently with a fork. With wet hands, lightly form the mixture into 8 meatballs.

◆ Prepare the plank for grilling according to the instructions on page 12. Place the meatballs on the toasted side of the plank. Close the lid and grill for 15 minutes, or until the meatballs are browned. Remove the meatballs from the grill and let them rest for 5 minutes before serving.

VEGETABLES & SIDES

I know this is probably not the correct way to introduce a chapter on vegetables, but I love meat. There are few dishes that make me happier than a perfectly grilled lamb chop. That being said, there is no denying that some of the best foods prepared on a grilling plank are vegetables. In fact, when I want to introduce someone to the amazing flavor plank grilling creates in a dish, I will often prepare a vegetable dish for them.

All the recipes in this chapter work best with cedarwood. Practically any vegetable tastes better plank-grilled, and here you'll find recipes for all the most common vegetables, including tomatoes, corn, bell peppers, potatoes (sweet and white), mushrooms, broccoli, artichokes, eggplant, asparagus, carrots, zucchini, and squash. If you want your kids to eat broccoli, try the Garlic and Lemon Broccoli (page 141) recipe first. It is simple to prepare and will make a vegetable convert out of almost anyone. Some other favorite recipes include Acorn Squash Glazed with Chipotle and Maple (page 148) and Carrots Glazed with Molasses and Miso (page 155).

When I don't feel like eating meat, I will prepare a plank-grilled vegetable recipe from this chapter and serve it with rice and beans for a complete meal. Even better, many of the stuffed vegetable recipes in this chapter are complete meals by themselves, since they include protein and grains all in one dish. The Zucchini Stuffed with Pesto Quinoa (page 154) is a favorite of mine because quinoa is a whole grain and a complete protein all in one. What's not to love about that?

Garlic and Lemon Broccoli

Plank-grilled broccoli is unlike any broccoli you've ever tasted. The florets caramelize and get crisp-tender during grilling, capturing the smoke and wood flavors better than most vegetables. The lemon and garlic provide the perfect amount of freshness and zing.

PLANK PREFERENCE:
Cedar or Alder

MAKES 4 SERVINGS

1 pound broccoli florets
2 tablespoons extra-virgin olive oil
Juice of ½ large lemon (about 2 tablespoons)
3 cloves garlic, minced
½ teaspoon kosher salt
¼ teaspoon freshly ground black pepper
¼ teaspoon crushed red pepper flakes

◆ Soak the plank for at least 1 hour and up to 24 hours.

◆ In a large bowl, combine the broccoli, oil, lemon juice, garlic, salt, pepper, and red pepper flakes and toss well.

◆ Prepare the plank for grilling according to the instructions on page 12. Spread the broccoli in a single layer on the toasted side of the plank. (If the broccoli does not fit in a single layer, then grill it in batches.) Close the lid and grill for 8 to 10 minutes, or until the broccoli is crisp-tender.

Tomato, Fennel, and Fresh Mozzarella Napoleons

PLANK PREFERENCE: Cedar

MAKES 6 SERVINGS

3 firm ripe tomatoes, halved

1 small fennel bulb (about ½ pound), cut into 6 slices

Zest of 1 medium lemon (about 1 tablespoon)

Juice of 1 medium lemon (about 3 tablespoons)

2 tablespoons extra-virgin olive oil

2 cloves garlic, minced

2 teaspoons sugar

4 large fresh basil leaves, sliced chiffonade (see note, page 43), plus more for garnish

1 teaspoon kosher salt

½ teaspoon freshly ground black pepper

6 ounces fresh mozzarella, cut into 6 slices

Tomatoes are in season from late June through August, making summer the best time of year to prepare this dish. Try to get perfectly ripe tomatoes that are roughly the same diameter as the fennel so that when you stack them, they look balanced. My friend Stacey Pruett Taddeucci was testing this recipe for me and used an aged, syrupy balsamic as a substitute for the marinade drizzle—I love that idea.

◆ Soak the plank for at least 1 hour and up to 24 hours.

◆ In a large bowl, combine the tomatoes, fennel, lemon zest and juice, oil, garlic, sugar, basil, salt, and pepper and toss to coat. Let marinate at room temperature for 30 minutes.

◆ Prepare the plank for grilling according to the instructions on page 12. Place the fennel slices and tomato halves, cut side down, on the toasted side of the plank, reserving the marinade. Close the lid and grill for 20 to 25 minutes, or until the vegetables are softened and lightly browned.

◆ Assemble the napoleons by placing a fennel slice on each of 6 plates. Top each with a slice of mozzarella and a tomato half. Drizzle with the reserved marinade and garnish with additional basil. Serve at room temperature.

Lemon-Herb Artichokes with Feta-Lemon Cream Sauce

PLANK PREFERENCE: Cedar

MAKES 6 TO 8 SERVINGS

4 medium artichokes
2 large lemons, halved
¼ cup kosher salt

For the marinade:
⅓ cup extra-virgin olive oil
Juice of 1 medium lemon (about
  3 tablespoons)
2 cloves garlic, minced
1 tablespoon chopped fresh
  flat-leaf parsley
1 tablespoon chopped fresh mint
1 tablespoon chopped fresh
  thyme
½ teaspoon kosher salt
¼ teaspoon freshly ground black
  pepper

If you're an artichoke fan, you'll find plank-grilled artichokes completely addictive. After soaking up the lemon-herb marinade, the artichokes are plank-grilled until they're crispy and smoky. The cedar wood gives them an extra sweet and spicy kick. The tangy sauce adds a fresh and creamy finish for dipping. The sauce can be prepared and refrigerated up to 1 day in advance.

• Slice the top third off of each artichoke and trim the brown part at the end of the stem. With a pair of kitchen scissors, trim the pointy tips off each leaf. Rub the cut sides of the artichokes with the lemons.

• Bring a large pot of water and the salt to a boil over high heat. Juice the lemons into the water and drop in the squeezed lemon halves. Reduce the heat to medium-high and carefully add the artichokes to the pot. Partially cover the pot and simmer until the artichokes are tender and their hearts can be pierced with a sharp knife, about 20 minutes. Drain the artichokes upside down on a plate until they are cool enough to handle.

- Meanwhile, prepare the marinade. In a large bowl, whisk together the oil, lemon juice, garlic, parsley, mint, thyme, salt, and pepper. Set aside.

- Next, prepare the sauce. In a medium bowl, whisk the sour cream, oil, feta, lemon juice, mint, salt, and pepper until combined. Refrigerate the sauce until the artichokes are ready to serve.

- Once the artichokes are cool enough to handle, quarter them and scoop out the prickly purple leaves and hairy choke. Place the artichoke quarters in the marinade and toss to coat. Marinate for 1 hour at room temperature, stirring occasionally.

- Prepare the plank for grilling according to the instructions on page 12. Place the artichoke quarters on the toasted side of the plank. Close the lid and grill for 15 minutes, or until the artichokes are lightly browned and crispy. Serve with the sauce on the side for dipping.

For the sauce:

½ cup sour cream

¼ cup extra-virgin olive oil

1 ounce feta, crumbled (about ¼ cup)

Juice of ½ large lemon (about 2 tablespoons)

1 tablespoon chopped fresh mint

¼ teaspoon kosher salt

¼ teaspoon freshly ground black pepper

Prosciutto-Wrapped Asparagus with Citrus Vinaigrette

My friends Jacki and Toby Leitch have a Meyer lemon tree in their backyard that yields the most copious amount of beautiful lemons I've ever seen on a tree. Every year, they generously share them with friends and neighbors. Here, I use them to make a wonderful vinaigrette for these prosciutto-wrapped asparagus spears. Meyer lemons taste a little sweeter than true lemons; the flavor is akin to a combination of mandarin orange and lemon. If Meyer lemons aren't in season, true lemons work great too. Be sure to zest the oranges and lemons before juicing them.

PLANK PREFERENCE: Cedar

MAKES 4 SERVINGS

18 stalks asparagus (about
   1 pound), tough ends removed
9 thin slices prosciutto (about
   4 ounces), halved lengthwise
1 teaspoon grated orange zest
1 tablespoon freshly squeezed
   orange juice
1 teaspoon grated Meyer lemon
   zest
1 tablespoon freshly squeezed
   Meyer lemon juice
1 tablespoon extra-virgin olive oil
¼ teaspoon kosher salt
¼ teaspoon freshly ground black
   pepper
1 tablespoon chopped fresh
   flat-leaf parsley

◆ Soak the plank for at least 1 hour and up to 24 hours.

◆ Wrap each asparagus stalk with ½ slice of prosciutto, leaving the tips of the asparagus exposed.

◆ In a small bowl, whisk together the orange zest and juice, lemon zest and juice, oil, salt, and pepper. Set aside.

◆ Prepare the plank for grilling according to the instructions on page 12. Place the asparagus spears on the toasted side of the plank in a single layer. (If the asparagus does not fit in a single layer, then grill them in batches.) Close the lid and grill for 15 minutes, or until the prosciutto is crisp. Transfer the asparagus to a platter. Drizzle with the citrus vinaigrette and garnish with the parsley. Serve warm or at room temperature.

Acorn Squash Glazed with Chipotle and Maple

PLANK PREFERENCE: Cedar

MAKES 4 SERVINGS

2 tablespoons unsalted butter

¼ cup maple syrup

2 canned chipotle chiles in adobo, finely chopped

Zest of 1 orange (about 2 tablespoons)

1 small acorn squash (about 1¼ pounds), cut into 12 wedges

½ teaspoon kosher salt

¼ teaspoon freshly ground black pepper

I love combining chipotle peppers with a sweet ingredient—the contrast in flavors leads to terrific results. The sauce can be prepared and refrigerated up to 2 days in advance and tossed with the squash right before you are ready to grill. For more information about chipotle chiles, see the note on page 103.

◆ Soak the plank for at least 1 hour and up to 24 hours.

◆ Melt the butter in a small saucepan over medium heat. Add the maple syrup, chipotles, and orange zest and cook, stirring often, for 2 minutes. Remove the chipotle sauce from the heat and let it cool for 10 minutes.

◆ Place the squash wedges in a large bowl and season with the salt and pepper. Drizzle them with the chipotle sauce, and toss until well coated.

◆ Prepare the plank for grilling according to the instructions on page 12. Place the squash wedges on their sides in a single layer on the toasted side of the plank. (If the squash does not fit in a single layer, then grill in batches.) Drizzle any remaining chipotle sauce from the bottom of the bowl over the squash. Close the lid and grill for 15 minutes, or until the squash is tender. Serve warm or at room temperature.

Potato and Kale Cakes with Spicy Harissa Sauce

Potatoes are culinary sponges—they soak up the flavors of every ingredient they come in contact with. In this case, they adopt the flavors of the wood plank and the smoke wonderfully. Kale is one of the healthiest vegetables around, and it pairs perfectly with the potatoes in both texture and flavor. If you prefer, though, spinach can be substituted for the kale. If you've never tried harissa, this is the perfect time to do so. It is a Tunisian hot chili sauce that can be quite spicy and is usually flavored with garlic, coriander, caraway, and cumin.

• Soak the plank for at least 1 hour and up to 24 hours.

• To prepare the sauce, in a small bowl, combine the mayonnaise and harissa. Refrigerate until the potato cakes are ready to serve.

• Place the potatoes and 1 teaspoon of the salt in a saucepan and add enough cold water to cover. Bring to a boil over medium-high heat. Simmer for 5 minutes, then add the kale and garlic. Continue cooking for 10 more minutes, or until the potatoes are tender. Drain the potatoes and kale in a colander, return them to the pot, and gently mash with a potato masher until the potatoes and garlic are smooth and incorporated with the kale.

• Add the Parmesan, green onions, oil, vinegar, pepper, and the remaining ½ teaspoon of salt to the potato mixture and stir until combined. Let the potato mixture cool to room temperature, about 20 minutes.

continued

continued

PLANK PREFERENCE:
Cedar or Alder

MAKES 4 SERVINGS

2 tablespoons mayonnaise

½ teaspoon harissa

1½ pounds russet potatoes, scrubbed and chopped into 1-inch cubes

1½ teaspoons kosher salt, divided

1 bunch kale (about 10 ounces), stemmed and chopped into 1-inch pieces

2 cloves garlic, sliced

¼ cup freshly grated Parmesan

2 green onions, thinly sliced

2 tablespoons extra-virgin olive oil

2 teaspoons white wine vinegar

¼ teaspoon freshly ground black pepper

Olive oil cooking spray

Coarse grind cornmeal, for sprinkling

- -

NOTE: Harissa can be found in most Middle Eastern markets or gourmet food stores. If you can't find harissa, it can be replaced with an Asian chili sauce like Sriracha or a standard hot sauce like Tabasco.

◆ Divide the potato mixture into 8 equal portions and, using your hands, shape each portion into a 1-inch-thick patty about 3 inches in diameter.

◆ Prepare the plank for grilling according to the instructions on page 12. Lightly spray the toasted side of the plank with the cooking spray and dust with cornmeal. Place the potato cakes in a single layer on the plank. (If the patties do not fit in a single layer, then grill them in batches.) Close the lid and grill for 15 minutes, or until the patties are lightly browned and the edges are crisp. Remove the potato cakes from the heat and let them cool for 10 minutes before topping with a dollop of the sauce. Serve warm or at room temperature.

Parmesan-Garlic Corn on the Cob

PLANK PREFERENCE: Cedar

MAKES 4 SERVINGS

¼ cup unsalted butter

Zest of 1 large lime (about 2 teaspoons)

Juice of 1 large lime (about 2 tablespoons)

2 cloves garlic, minced

1 teaspoon chili powder

½ teaspoon kosher salt

¼ teaspoon freshly ground black pepper

4 ears corn, husks and silk removed

½ cup freshly grated Parmesan

I love corn on the cob, and I'm always looking for new ways to prepare it. If you're in the same boat, try this version. It is inspired by the corn on the cob sold in Mexico by street vendors, with flavors of spicy chili and tangy lime. The street vendors grill theirs, too, but this version has the added benefit of being infused with the flavor of cedar wood. The Parmesan cheese forms a nice crispy crust to offset the juicy corn kernels.

◆ Soak the plank for at least 1 hour and up to 24 hours.

◆ Melt the butter in a small saucepan over medium heat. Add the lime zest and juice, garlic, chili powder, salt, and pepper and cook, stirring often, for 2 minutes. Remove the butter mixture from the heat and let it cool for 10 minutes.

◆ Brush the corn with the butter mixture. Sprinkle each corn cob with 2 tablespoons of the Parmesan, making sure the cobs are evenly coated with cheese.

◆ Prepare the plank for grilling according to the instructions on page 12. Place the corn on the toasted side of the plank. Close the lid and grill for 20 minutes, or until the corn is golden and crisp. Serve immediately.

Zucchini Stuffed with Pesto Quinoa

PLANK PREFERENCE: Cedar

MAKES 4 SERVINGS

½ cup quinoa

1 cup water

¾ teaspoon kosher salt, divided

1 (7-ounce) package pesto

1 large tomato, cut into ¼-inch
   dice

3 ounces mozzarella, grated
   (about 1 cup)

2 tablespoons toasted pine nuts

4 medium zucchini, halved
   lengthwise

¼ teaspoon freshly ground black
   pepper

1 tablespoon freshly grated
   Parmesan

Quinoa is a seed native to Peru, and is considered a super food because it's a complete protein and has twice as much fiber as any other grain. I could go on and on about the benefits of quinoa, but the most important thing is that it tastes delicious, with a nutty flavor similar to brown rice. Unless your quinoa is labeled as pre-washed, make sure to rinse it well before cooking to remove any bitter sediment.

◆ Soak the plank for at least 1 hour and up to 24 hours.

◆ Place the quinoa in a small saucepan over medium-high heat. Toast for 5 minutes, stirring occasionally, until it begins to smell nutty and fragrant. Add the water and ½ teaspoon of the salt and bring to a boil. Reduce the heat to low, cover, and cook for 15 minutes, or until the water has all been absorbed and the quinoa is tender and fluffy. Remove the pan from the heat and let the quinoa cool to room temperature.

◆ In a large bowl, combine the quinoa, pesto, tomato, mozzarella, and pine nuts.

◆ Scoop the pulp from the zucchini halves with a spoon. Discard the pulp and season the zucchini with the pepper and the remaining ¼ teaspoon of salt. Spoon the quinoa mixture evenly among the zucchini, pressing the mixture firmly into the hollowed-out halves. Sprinkle with the Parmesan.

◆ Prepare the plank for grilling according to the instructions on page 12. Place the zucchini halves, stuffed sides up, on the toasted side of the plank. Close the lid and grill for 20 minutes, or until the zucchini are tender when pierced with a fork.

Carrots Glazed with Molasses and Miso

Miso is one of those ingredients that is often associated with just one specific preparation (in this case, miso soup), but it can enhance so many other dishes, especially sauces. Dressed-up with molasses and orange zest, these carrots really shine when plank-grilled and have a wonderfully smoky, sweet flavor that matches their natural sweetness.

PLANK PREFERENCE: Cedar

MAKES 4 SERVINGS

2 tablespoons unsalted butter
¼ cup molasses
2 tablespoons white miso (see note, page 76)
2 teaspoons grated orange zest
1 teaspoon freshly grated ginger
4 or 5 large carrots (about 1 pound)
1 teaspoon toasted sesame seeds (optional)

• Soak the plank for at least 1 hour and up to 24 hours.

• Melt the butter in a small saucepan over medium heat. Add the molasses, miso, orange zest, and ginger and cook, stirring often, for 2 minutes. Remove the molasses mixture from the heat and let it cool for 10 minutes.

• Meanwhile, peel the carrots and slice them diagonally into ½-inch-thick pieces. Place the carrots in a large bowl. Drizzle them with the molasses mixture, and toss until well coated.

• Prepare the plank for grilling according to the instructions on page 12. Place the carrots in a single layer on the toasted side of the plank. (If the carrots do not fit in a single layer, then grill in batches.) Drizzle any remaining molasses mixture from the bowl over the carrots. Close the lid and grill for 20 minutes, or until the carrots are tender. Arrange the carrots on a serving dish and garnish with the sesame seeds. Serve warm or at room temperature.

Spicy Sweet Potato Wedges

PLANK PREFERENCE: Cedar

MAKES 4 SERVINGS

2 medium sweet potatoes (about
    1¼ pounds), peeled
2 tablespoons extra-virgin olive oil
2 tablespoons packed brown
    sugar
1 teaspoon chili powder
½ teaspoon dried thyme
1 teaspoon kosher salt
½ teaspoon freshly ground
    black pepper

My friend Susan Lockwood likes to prepare these as fries, and cuts them smaller and thinner so they get more crisp on the plank. My husband prefers them as wedges, my son loves them both ways, and that is the great thing about this dish—either way, it is delicious and so simple to make. The oil and spice mixture can be prepared earlier in the day and combined with the sweet potatoes right before grilling.

◆ Soak the plank for at least 1 hour and up to 24 hours.

◆ Cut each potato lengthwise into 1-inch-wide wedges and place them in a large bowl. Sprinkle with the oil, brown sugar, chili powder, thyme, salt, and pepper and toss until the wedges are well coated.

◆ Prepare the plank for grilling according to the instructions on page 12. Place the potato wedges in a single layer on the toasted side of the plank. (If your potatoes do not fit in a single layer, then grill in batches.) Close the lid and grill for 15 to 20 minutes, or until the potato wedges are crispy on the outside and tender on the inside. Serve warm or at room temperature.

Open-Faced Tofu and Avocado Sandwiches

My sister Lamia Epperson has been trying to get me to eat more tofu, thinking I might start eating less meat if I do. After trying this sandwich, I'm not sure why I needed so much convincing—it is seriously tasty and satisfies on all levels! It's messy, and you need a fork and knife to eat it, but don't let that stop you. Tofu soaks up any flavor you mix it with, and it responds so well to plank grilling. I prefer my tofu creamy—I think it contrasts nicely with the crunchy cucumber, crusty bread, and crispy cilantro. If, like Lamia, you prefer your tofu a little denser, just let it sit for 30 minutes before marinating it, instead of the 15 minutes this recipe calls for.

---

* Soak the plank for at least 1 hour and up to 24 hours.

* Place the tofu slices on a plate lined with a double layer of paper towels, lay another double layer of paper towels on top, and press gently for 10 seconds. Discard the damp paper towels. Line the plate with a fresh double layer of paper towels, place the tofu on it, and let the tofu sit for 15 minutes. Transfer the tofu slices to an 8-inch-square baking pan.

* In a small bowl, combine the soy sauce, oil, miso, ginger, garlic, sugar, pepper, and 2 tablespoons of the lime juice. Whisk until the sugar dissolves and pour the marinade over the tofu. Turn the tofu to coat both sides and let it marinate at room temperature for 1 hour, turning halfway through.

* In another small bowl, combine the carrots, mayonnaise, and Sriracha. Set aside.

continued

PLANK PREFERENCE: Cedar

MAKES 4 SERVINGS

1-pound block extra-firm tofu, cut lengthwise into 4 (½-inch-thick) slices
¼ cup low-sodium soy sauce
1 tablespoon toasted sesame oil
1 tablespoon white miso (see the note on page 76)
1 tablespoon freshly grated ginger
3 cloves garlic, minced
2 teaspoons sugar
½ teaspoon freshly ground black pepper
Juice of 1½ large limes (about 3 tablespoons), divided
¼ cup grated carrots
¼ cup mayonnaise
1 teaspoon Sriracha sauce
1 avocado
4 (⅓-inch-thick) slices rustic bread
1 English cucumber, cut diagonally into (¼-inch-thick) slices
1 cup cilantro sprigs
1 tablespoon chopped fresh cilantro leaves, for garnish

◆ Peel the avocado, remove the pit, and slice it into 12 pieces. In a small bowl, combine the avocado slices with the remaining 1 tablespoon of lime juice.

◆ Prepare the plank for grilling according to the instructions on page 12. Place the tofu slices in a single layer on the toasted side of the plank, reserving the marinade. Close the lid and grill for 12 minutes, or until the tofu is golden. Remove the plank from the heat. Grill the bread slices on the grill until toasted.

◆ Spread about 1 tablespoon of the carrot mixture on each piece of bread. Top each piece with 3 slices of avocado, 3 slices of cucumber, ¼ cup of the cilantro sprigs, and 1 slice of the grilled tofu. Drizzle with the reserved marinade and garnish with the chopped cilantro.

Creole Stuffed Eggplant

PLANK PREFERENCE: Cedar

MAKES 4 SERVINGS

4 Japanese eggplants, or
   2 medium eggplants,
   halved lengthwise
1 pound bulk Italian pork sausage
3 tablespoons extra-virgin olive
   oil, divided
1 medium red bell pepper,
   chopped
2 stalks celery, chopped
1 medium onion, chopped
1 tablespoon chopped garlic
1 cup chopped mushrooms
1 teaspoon dried thyme
½ teaspoon cayenne pepper
½ teaspoon kosher salt, plus
   more for sprinkling
¼ teaspoon freshly ground black
   pepper
1 cup fresh bread crumbs (see
   note, page 126)
1 cup freshly grated Parmesan,
   divided
3 ounces mozzarella, grated
   (about 1 cup)

If you like stuffed eggplant, you need to try this version. Plank-grilling the stuffed eggplant on cedar infuses it with a sweetness and smokiness and turns this vegetable into an exhilarating entrée or side dish.

◆ Soak the plank for at least 1 hour and up to 24 hours.

◆ Using a spoon, hollow out the center of each eggplant half to make a boatlike shell about ¼ inch thick. Reserve the pulp. Sprinkle the interiors of the shells with a few pinches of salt and invert them on paper towels to drain. Finely chop the eggplant pulp and set aside.

◆ While the eggplants are draining, prepare the stuffing. In a large skillet, brown the sausage over medium-high heat until cooked through. Using a slotted spoon, transfer the sausage to a medium bowl and set aside. Add 2 tablespoons of the oil to the skillet and sauté the bell pepper, celery, onion, and garlic until soft, about 10 minutes. Reduce the heat to medium and add the eggplant pulp and mushrooms to the skillet. Cook until most of the liquid has evaporated, 7 to 10 minutes Add the thyme, cayenne, salt, and pepper and stir to combine. Set aside to cool.

◆ Pat the eggplant shells dry. Lightly brush each shell with the remaining 1 tablespoon of oil. Transfer the vegetable mixture to a large bowl and stir in the sausage, bread crumbs, and ½ cup of the Parmesan.

◆ In a small bowl, mix the remaining ½ cup of Parmesan and the mozzarella and set aside.

◆ Prepare the plank for grilling according to the instructions on page 12. Spoon the stuffing into the eggplant shells and place them on the toasted side of the plank. Close the lid and grill for 20 to 25 minutes for Japanese eggplants or 35 to 40 minutes for medium eggplants, or until the eggplants are tender. Open the grill lid and sprinkle the eggplants with the cheese. Close the lid and grill for an additional 3 minutes, or until the cheese is melted.

Green Beans, Tomatoes, and Feta

PLANK PREFERENCE: Cedar

MAKES 4 SERVINGS

1 tablespoon plus ½ teaspoon
  kosher salt, divided
1 pound green beans, trimmed
1 pint cherry tomatoes, halved
1 tablespoon extra-virgin olive oil
½ teaspoon freshly ground black
  pepper
2 ounces feta, crumbled (about
  ½ cup)
¼ cup chopped fresh basil
¼ cup chopped fresh mint
Juice of 1 medium lemon (about
  3 tablespoons)

I created this dish for my friend, Katja Pollman, who loves green beans but was looking for a new way to prepare them. Katja is from Germany and grew up eating her green beans with bacon and cider vinegar. This dish is so simple, yet the flavors that the beans and tomatoes get from plank grilling are intense and smoky, and the lemon, herbs, and feta give it a fresh, Mediterranean twist. For a quick preparation, the green beans can be parboiled earlier in the day and stored in the refrigerator until you're ready to grill them. Parboiling is a cooking technique in which food items are partially cooked in boiling water, then fully cooked using another method of cooking—in this case, plank grilling.

◆ Bring a large pot of water to a boil over high heat. Have a large bowl of ice water ready. Add 1 tablespoon of the salt and the green beans to the pot and boil for 4 minutes (be careful not to overcook the beans at this point since you will be plank-grilling them later). Using tongs or a spider strainer, transfer the beans to the ice water to stop the cooking. Once the beans are completely cool, pour them into a colander, dry out the large bowl, pat the beans dry with a paper towel, and return them to the bowl.

◆ Toss the beans with the tomatoes, oil, pepper, and the remaining ½ teaspoon of salt.

◆ Prepare the plank for grilling according to the instructions on page 12. Spread the green beans and tomatoes in a single layer on the toasted side of the plank. Close the lid and grill for 10 to 15 minutes, or until the tomatoes and beans have caramelized. Return them to the large bowl.

◆ Add the feta, basil, mint, and lemon juice and toss until well coated. Taste for seasoning, adding more salt or pepper if desired. Serve warm or at room temperature.

Tomatoes Stuffed with Shrimp and Couscous

I come from a family that loves to cook, and everyone is good at it, from my parents to my brother, sister, aunts, uncles, and cousins. You are guaranteed a great meal in any of their homes. We love our fresh vegetables any way they can be prepared, and if it can be stuffed, my mom will stuff it. Everything from cabbage, zucchini, peppers, eggplant—you name it. One of my favorite things to make is stuffed tomatoes. The small, Moroccan-style couscous works best in this recipe.

◆ Soak the plank for at least 1 hour and up to 24 hours.

◆ Cut the tops off of the tomatoes. Scoop out the pulp and discard it. Sprinkle the interior shells of the tomatoes with a few pinches of salt and invert them on paper towels to drain.

◆ While the tomatoes are draining, prepare the stuffing. In a large bowl, whisk together the dry mustard, oil, balsamic vinegar, shallot, garlic, and basil. Add the shrimp, couscous, salt, and pepper and stir to combine. Fill the tomato cavities with the couscous mixture.

◆ Prepare the plank for grilling according to the instructions on page 12. Place the stuffed tomatoes on the toasted side of the plank. Close the lid and grill for 10 to 15 minutes, or until the tomatoes are slightly softened. Open the grill lid and sprinkle the goat cheese over the tomatoes. Close the lid and grill for an additional 2 minutes, or until the cheese is melted. The tomatoes will soften as they grill, so use a slotted spoon to carefully remove them from the plank.

PLANK PREFERENCE:
Cedar or Alder

MAKES 4 SERVINGS

4 large (3-inch-wide) ripe tomatoes
½ teaspoon dry mustard
¼ cup extra-virgin olive oil
1 tablespoon balsamic vinegar
1 shallot, minced
2 cloves garlic, minced
1 tablespoon chopped fresh basil
1 cup cooked bay shrimp (about ½ pound)
1 cup cooked couscous, cooled
½ teaspoon kosher salt
¼ teaspoon freshly ground black pepper
4 ounces goat cheese, crumbled (about 1 cup)

Southwest Stuffed Bell Peppers

PLANK PREFERENCE:
Cedar or Alder

MAKES 4 SERVINGS

4 large red or green bell peppers

3 tablespoons tomato paste

¾ cup pilsner-style beer (such as Budweiser)

¾ cup ketchup

2 tablespoons extra-virgin olive oil

1 medium onion, chopped

3 cloves garlic, minced

1 pound ground beef

1 cup frozen corn kernels, thawed

1 cup cooked white rice

1½ teaspoons kosher salt

½ teaspoon freshly ground black pepper

½ teaspoon ground cumin

½ teaspoon ancho chili powder

1 cup shredded Pepper Jack cheese

This is one of those dishes I prefer plank-grilled instead of baked, which is the traditional method. Plank grilling really showcases the smoky taste of fire-roasted bell peppers. You can use red or green bell peppers in this recipe—they both work wonderfully.

◆ Soak the plank for at least 1 hour and up to 24 hours.

◆ Cut the tops off of the peppers and discard the stems. Chop enough of the pepper tops to measure 1 cup. Remove and discard the seeds and membranes from the peppers and set aside.

◆ In a medium bowl, combine the tomato paste and beer, stirring well with a whisk. Add the ketchup, mix well, and set aside.

◆ In a large skillet, heat the oil over medium heat. Add the chopped pepper tops, onion, and garlic and sauté for 7 to 10 minutes, or until the vegetables have softened. Add the ground beef and sauté together until the beef is completely cooked. Drain the fat from the pan. Add the corn and rice and cook for 1 minute. Add the salt, pepper, cumin, chili powder, and half of the ketchup mixture. Stir well. Remove the stuffing from the heat and allow it to cool slightly.

◆ Prepare the plank for grilling according to the instructions on page 12. Spoon the stuffing into the peppers and place them on the toasted side of the plank. Spoon the remaining half of the ketchup mixture over the peppers. Close the lid and grill for 15 to 20 minutes, or until the peppers are just softened and lightly charred. Open the grill lid and sprinkle the cheese over the peppers. Close the lid and grill for an additional 2 minutes, or until the cheese is melted.

ACKNOWLEDGMENTS

Writing cookbooks is a collaborative effort and I'm incredibly grateful to so many people who helped and supported me. First and foremost, a huge thank-you to my husband, Roland, and my son, Andrew. No matter what I serve them, they think it's the most delicious thing they've ever eaten. They believe in me always and that unconditional love and support means the world to me.

A big thank-you to my friend Laura Howell who was by my side from the beginning to the end, suggesting and tweaking, until each recipe was exactly right. You inspired me with your creative ideas and helped make this project so much fun.

I would also like to thank my friend Susan Lockwood who shared her vast knowledge of charcoal grills with me, and meticulously provided step-by-step instructions on the best way to plank grill with a charcoal grill.

There's also a dear and valued group of friends and family who, after I wrote each recipe, took them home and tested them to make sure they worked. Odette Abukhater. Betsy Black. Susan Lockwood. Lisa Berman Edmunds. Stacey Pruett Taddeucci. Kristin and Mike Ross. Jacki and Toby Leitch. Laura and Brock Howell. Lamia Epperson. From the bottom of my heart, thank you all so much.

I've been with Sasquatch Books since my first book, and I want to thank the entire Sasquatch team for all the help and guidance they've provided me. And to my wonderful agent, Jennifer Unter, thank you for taking care of business so I could enjoy the fun parts of writing a cookbook.

And especially, thanks to my brother Sam Nassar, who introduced me to plank grilling. I love to cook, and I love to write. He encouraged me to combine both passions together to create recipes and write cookbooks. I love you.

INDEX

Photograph by Andrew Guillen

DINA GUILLEN is the co-author of the cookbook, *Cooking Club*. She has been interviewed and profiled by *Cooking Light* magazine, Martha Stewart Living Radio, the *Washington Post*, the *Sacramento Bee*, and numerous television programs. Guillen has written and developed several recipes for *Cooking Light* magazine, as well as for her own website, Dina-Guillen.com.